SOCIAL MEDIA LEADERSHIP

HOW TO GET OFF THE BENCH
AND INTO THE GAME

By

Michael F. Lewis

LEIGH WALKER BOOKS

Library of Congress Control Number: 2011932538

ISBN 978-0-9832431-2-0

Printed in the United States of America

This book is dedicated to my lovely wife Jane, to my wonderful kids, Tracey, Betsy, Michael, Jennifer and Emily, and to my grandchildren, Hannah and Alex.

Acknowledgments

I would like to express my utmost appreciation and thanks to my editor and collaborator, Cynthia Parks. She was all in on this project from day one and encouraged me to write in my own style and to be honest and authentic in presenting many of my firsthand experiences.

I would also like to thank my ILD and Social Strategy 1 staffs for their help in organizing and presenting the contents of this book. I am most grateful to Steve Ennen, President of Social Strategy 1. He has been a remarkable source of knowledge and a great sounding board throughout the process of writing this book, particularly on the topic of monitoring and measuring. Special thanks also to Ilona Olayan, Dennis Stoutenburgh, and Fred Lloyd for all their assistance and contributions. Their collective knowledge and input was invaluable.

My son, Michael, and my daughter, Jennifer, have taught me many of the practical applications of

Facebook, Twitter, and other platforms. They were also very helpful and supportive of the old man during the writing of the book.

Ed Brown at Burr & Forman did a magnificent job in describing social media issues from both a lawyer's and a client's perspective. My sincere thanks and appreciation to Ed for recognizing the value of this content and doing a great job of presenting it in such a straightforward and understandable manner.

I am grateful to Robert Ball of OfficeArrow.com for his detailed thoughts in Chapter 5 and for his help on the content presented on online communities.

Eric Bradlow, K. P. Chao Professor of Marketing at The Wharton School, gets credit for first proposing this book. Many thanks, Eric. I hope we did it justice! Many thanks, too, to all of the other faculty and staff associated with the wonderful alumni outreach programs at Wharton.

Mike Lewis

Foreword

The idea for writing this book was presented to me in the fall of 2009 by Professor Eric Bradlow of The Wharton School. My first response was, "What in the world are you thinking?" I certainly didn't see myself as an author. But Eric felt that we had a great story to tell, and in thinking more about the idea of a book, I realized that we actually had experienced success in using social media to grow and improve our business and that our story might really be of value if it were shared with other companies, executives, and entrepreneurs. So, after more than another year of contemplation, we decided to go for it and to write a friendly book that might eliminate some of the confusion that is associated with all that is social media.

As I spoke with businesspeople like myself, I realized that many of them were intimidated by the language and terminology that is associated with social media and they often felt like they were getting an earful of jargon. They were confused by the discussions that focused on digital media and technology and they wondered about the practical applications of platforms they associated with their kids or younger peers. They expressed difficulty in being able to sort through this noise and confusion and understand how they could use the fundamentals of social media to grow their business.

Moving you out of all this noise and traffic is the main focus of this book. First of all, I'm a businessman and entrepreneur, not an acknowledged social media expert. I'm one of you—just a regular guy who tries to focus every day on how to build and grow my business. All of the content of the book is presented from that perspective, so there's not a lot of technical mumbo jumbo. If you can't understand what the experts are telling you, this book may be a useful reference tool on the fundamentals of social media. The details of our hands-on experience, and the experience of others, will demonstrate ways your business can make money by utilizing social media initiatives. My expectation is that you will come away with several ideas that you will find valuable and practical.

We started this effort knowing that it would be impossible to hit everyone's sweet spot. The range of readers' social media experience will be varied, and some will have an even greater familiarity with certain platforms and applications than we do. We believe, however, that our discussion of the impact of social media on corporate governance and financial reporting does break some new ground and hope that even the most social savvy readers will gain insight into this emerging trend.

My hope is that throughout the book you will be able to sense my enthusiasm for the changes and opportunities that social media brings to business from the largest company to the one-person business. Even though I have quite a few years on the whiz kids of social media, I'm proof positive that an old dog can learn new tricks!

x

Contents

Chapter 1. From the Pew to the Pulpit

I wasn't always a believer, let alone a preacher, for the business opportunities inherent in social media and social networking. I wasn't even in the choir. To be perfectly truthful, until only a few years ago, I was sound asleep in a back pew. The process that woke me up, and has since made me practically an evangelist for encouraging others to participate in these exciting new trends, only began in early 2007. It was a rather rude awakening, for me and for my company. But the process, I suspect, was not terribly different from that encountered by many companies in the last few years. One that could surprise any organization not already paying serious attention to all aspects of social media and e-commerce.

I've been a serial entrepreneur for twenty-five years. Several of my ventures were born, and grew up, in the Internet Age and utilize many of the advantages that the digital revolution has opened up for e-commerce. ILD Corp is one of them. Our company at the time was about eleven years old. We were a leading payment processor for transactions between merchants and consumers. Through contractual relationships with local telephone companies, ILD enabled consumers to charge the products and services of hundreds of merchants directly to their phone bills.

Now, very few industries have experienced the changes that telecommunications has gone through in the last decade or so, and at ILD we'd had our own share of evolving and adapting. We'd grown from a five-person start-up to more than 300 employees with over $100 million in annual revenues. We hadn't done it by being afraid to embrace new technological trends. But in 2007 our social media awareness was pretty much in the Stone Age.

I knew, of course, about online sites like Facebook and MySpace. These were places where kids connected to share jokes and pictures, mostly to gossip, and mostly about each other. I knew, too, that some networking sites, like LinkedIn, had started to form, where grown-ups shared business contacts and product information. But we didn't participate in any of these. We didn't blog, network, share in any professional communities, or have any online presence at all beyond the corporate face of our website. Social media was not on our minds, or anywhere on our marketing horizon.

The wake-up call came innocently enough, on an ordinary Monday, when a curious employee put the name of our company into a Google search window. The results of that search sent shockwaves throughout the organization. Not only had Google found us, but what it had found was ugly. There were multiple instances of consumers complaining about unauthorized charges and billing methods posted on blogs and message boards and consumer complaint sites. Some of the comments had already inspired local newspaper articles or other media investigations. The content of the comments reflected simple misunderstandings, as well as some outright factual inaccuracies, but they were peppered with exclamation marks, and their tone was anything but friendly. Here's just one example to illustrate how bad it was:

> You put a charge of $16 on my phone bill!!!!Shame on you. I did not approve of that. So, our local TV station came out, took video and statements and aired it, telling all about your crooked business. I called my telephone company and had them put a block on 3rd party bills. The FTC will hear about it too. They should put you out of business!!!!!!!

Our initial reaction was disappointment and denial. These people weren't talking about us! This wasn't our culture. Not the way *we* did business.

We had always monitored our business closely. Month over month the statistics showed that inquiries were in the 1.8% range. This was consistent with our business and well within the payment-processing industry norm. What we *hadn't* been tracking was this new world of Web 2.0. We didn't have the stats for that. We had also invested millions of dollars in what we thought was an effective state-of-the-art call center operation, but most of these folks hadn't even bothered with that step before going public with their complaints. We didn't want to believe any of this. But we had to. The customer names were genuine, and so was the frustration. Clearly, this was serious.

I brought together our senior staff and we began to brainstorm, trying to figure out what to do. One possible strategy was simply to fight fire with fire—to outblog them, if we could. We discarded that one pretty quickly. It didn't address the main issue anyway. We were being misunderstood by the consumers because our merchants had changed their marketing methods. It was now clear to us that trying to push consumers to a call center for resolution wasn't acceptable to them anymore. We needed significant change or the entire reputation of the company that we had worked so hard to cultivate would be permanently damaged.

As our thinking evolved, we gradually realized that if our customers could reach out to us so easily, there had to be methods for us to reach out, too, but in a positive, constructive way. If consumers could light us up like this on the Internet, we should be able to solve their issues on the Internet, too.

We reviewed every part of our process and instituted a set of best practices for ourselves and our merchants to ensure that we were placing the consumer first. We set up an offsite customer forum, inviting the phone companies, all merchants of ILD, and authorities like Forbes publisher Rich Karlgaard, author of *Wall Street Journal* best seller *Life 2.0* and an expert on the new interactive Web, to participate. By bringing this group of business leaders, industry experts, and merchants together, we hoped to redefine how consumers were marketed to, and how they could be supported throughout the buying process. We recognized that having a call center as the sole customer service channel was no longer feasible.

Our first action step was to update ILD's website with a consumer-centric focus. We developed the payment industry's first self-help application, giving consumers the ability to learn more about specific transactions and the merchants charging them, and enabling them to take action on their own behalf. Consumers could submit inquiries about unrecognized charges, verify credit requests, and find a fast track to canceling services. The self-help application yielded almost immediate results. We were able to handle customer issues quicker, and more effectively, and the volume at our call center also dropped. Our customers were still talking "off" our site, but not so frequently, and the rhetoric had cooled down. One comment even confirmed it:

> I can see from the Web that your company has become quite "popular" again and am hoping that your posts were sincere.

We were pleased with our new customer service tool and cautiously optimistic about our new approach, but we'd been permanently rocked out of complacency. We now began to allocate resources for monitoring what was being said about our company on the Internet and to think seriously about how to manage our reputation in this new era of what seemed like not-so-sociable media.

By the spring of 2007 I had joined the choir. I had conceded that the customer could control the message now and that social media wasn't just for kids anymore. But my next big consciousness-raising experience came in March when my wife and I traveled to Philadelphia to attend a conference hosted by my alma mater, The Wharton School. At that event I met and developed an instant rapport with Eric Bradlow, the K. P. Chao Professor of Marketing, who would become co-director of the Wharton Interactive Media Initiative. The association with WIMI would prove surprisingly valuable to us, but there was another surprise in store. In one of the early sessions, on the theme of business development, another marketing professor made a statement that astonished me. The professor told us that, if he were the head of a Fortune 500 company, he wouldn't spend a dime on traditional marketing. His money, he said, would go to social media.

Now, that was an eye-opener, particularly in light of our own recent experiences at ILD. I had definitely acknowledged that the social media phenomena was a problem that had to be reckoned with, but I still perceived it as a problem—a nuisance, really—in that we now had to devote time and resources to efforts that we hadn't planned for, and didn't really know how to capitalize on. But here was the suggestion that social media should be perceived as opportunity, not as obstacle. Maybe old Jonathan Swift was wrong on this one. Maybe you *could* make a silk purse out of a sow's ear. Wasn't that, after all, what entrepreneurs were supposed to do?

Over the next few months, I began to think seriously about how we could actually use social media to promote our own brands. One of our brands at ILD, our RollCall Business Conferencing Service, seemed particularly well suited to a social community environment. The only problem was that there wasn't a community environment available for us to successfully promote our services and our brand. Another obstacle, another opportunity.

During the process of searching for a social networking site for RollCall to partner with, we concluded that a number of the decision makers who bought conferencing services fell into the categories of office professionals and small business owners. In communicating further with this group, we discovered that they felt a strong need and desire to collaborate online with other professionals, that they were receptive to content and information that would increase their productivity, and that they were often responsible for the purchasing of office products and services.

Over a short period we surveyed this group and decided that we would pursue this as a business opportunity. I sought out an old colleague, Robert Ball, who readily jumped in, and by late summer of 2007, we founded the OfficeArrow.com site for small businesses and office professionals to collaborate, to access expert and user-generated content, and to conduct commerce.

While OfficeArrow's success as a professional social networking site was exciting, its business model was still new. As we continued to grow the company, we began thinking about putting a group together to share ideas on the business application of social media and networking. In February 2009, we decided to organize a small summit with our friends at the Wharton Interactive Media Initiative. This initiative was becoming the academic epicenter for social media research at Wharton, bringing together faculty, students, and corporate sponsors to gain and share knowledge in all applications of social media.

In September 2009, OfficeArrow and the WIMI co-sponsored the first Lift Summit, which brought together more than one hundred national thought leaders to share updates on recent developments and best practices. We were fortunate to have Erik Qualman, author of *Socialnomics*, and Eric Bradlow as keynote speakers. The event was very high-energy and produced a number of great ideas and connections.

One prominent area of discussion was the role of listening and monitoring software platforms designed to assist companies in keeping up with what's being said about them online. With ILD's president, Dennis

Stoutenburgh, we began to brainstorm about developing a platform of our own that would combine a number of these software applications and couple this with the strategic knowledge that we had gained through ILD's own experience. The net result was the concept for our Social Strategy1 initiative.

In April 2010, we formally launched Social Strategy1, a managed social media monitoring and strategy service, to help companies capitalize on the opportunities that are available on the increasingly open and social Web. By combining the best available tools for social media listening and engagement with our one-of-a-kind reporting platform, we committed to providing constant monitoring of brand conversations for our clients, as well as consultation by professional analysts who know how to apply that gathered information to core business initiatives. I'm pleased to report great initial success from this venture and the interaction with our client/partners has greatly contributed to the content of this book.

With the launch of Social Strategy1, we decided to host a second summit in the fall in Atlanta, Georgia. Lift Summit 2010 continued to reflect our conviction that social media strategies and tactics can "lift" sales and profoundly influence the bottom line. This second event brought together an extraordinary lineup of business owners, C-level executives, social influencers, and professors, as well as internationally acclaimed social media experts to discuss how to make money using social media. Much of what we have learned at our various Lift Summits will be shared with you in these pages.

At our last summit, I got the opportunity to take the pulpit, if you will. I welcomed participants, thanked our terrific sponsors, and took a few minutes to tell the story about my amazing odyssey as an entrepreneur. The thrust of my remarks was the acknowledgment that it's been a remarkable experience so far, but things are just getting started. My experience, my instincts, and everything we've learned from research and active participants tell me that we've only seen a glimpse of how social media will revolutionize the way we do business.

Conclusion

Recent business headlines tell us that Goldman Sachs is investing $500 million in Facebook at a $100 billion valuation. Groupon, which declined a $6 billion buyout offer from Google in December 2010, has raised almost $1 billion in new capital in 2011. I don't know about you, but these seem to me like some pretty serious bets on companies that only got started a few years ago. The Facebook and Groupon examples, however, are but two indications of the changes, already well underway, in how people will communicate, interact, and conduct business in the future. Those changes will be as dramatic as they are rapid. They will happen with or without your participation. How your business adapts to them will determine your success, possibly your survival.

I sense that many executives are wary and perplexed at the thought of jumping into the social media fray. Things are happening so fast that there is certainly the possibility of succumbing to information overload— or, to put it another way, the old "paralysis from analysis." But opportunities abound in the new social landscape, and the learning curve is well worth its mastery.

The goal of this book, then, is to present both a comprehensive assessment of the current environment and to offer a roadmap for developing strategies that your company, whether large or small, can immediately deploy and benefit from. My hope is that, by sharing what we have learned by trial and error, as well as the best practices and successful initiatives of other companies, you can go, and grow, more confidently in the new world of social media. This is a story of a real company that is not afraid of making commitments with its money to be on the front lines of this business phenomenon.

In accepting the challenge to adapt to the new realities of social media communication and engagement, you may be charting an entirely new course for your company. I'm convinced that it's one you'll find not only exciting but profitable.

Chapter 2. Chatter That Matters

To many people, Facebook *is* social media, and there are some pretty good reasons for that perception. Facebook's statistics are not merely impressive, they are almost unfathomable:

- 200 million users in 2009
- 275 million *new* registered users in 2010
- 650 million active users in 2011
- 35 million users who update their status every day
- 30 billion content pieces shared monthly

Given Facebook's growth and its almost ubiquitous reputation, it can be pretty hard to disabuse folks of the idea that there's much more to social media than just Facebook. (The Academy Awards recently won

by *The Social Network* don't help much in that regard.)
But for all its power and reach, Facebook is only one
application and only one manifestation of the social
media phenomenon.

In its broadest and simplest definition, social
media is any form of online communication that not only
"talks" to you, as traditional media like newspapers or
radio might be said to do, but also allows you to talk
back, facilitating a dialogue. In the old paradigm, which
some have taken to calling Web 1.0, communication was
a one-way process. As Web 2.0 has settled in, we see a
larger, much more inclusive phenomenon, where
communication becomes connectedness, sharing,
location-based engagement, and buying and selling
across a global network.

Social media channels include dynamically
generated blogs and microblogs, social and professional
networking sites, social gaming, bookmarking sites,
location-based services, and those that allow for sharing
of photographs, videos, and slide presentations or other
content. As the individual islands in this social media
stream become more populated, they become networks,
benefitting from "network effects," analogous to those of
a telephone network. As more and more users join, the
value of the network increases to those users by giving
them more people to "talk" to, thus extending their

sphere of influence.

When you begin to combine big network numbers with the fact that these conversations happen in real time, you can get powerful, and fast, effects. We know, for example, that online chatter can negatively affect stock prices.[1] We saw how quickly a Facebook page galvanized sentiment to bring Betty White out of retirement. We've seen how today's social buying coupons can fill a restaurant by the end of the day. And think you can dash out for the morning paper in your birthday suit? Think again. By dinnertime, you could be "exposed" to ten million viewers.

In the United States, where 46 percent of Internet users say they use sites like Facebook and MySpace, social media is already a factor in nearly every facet of American life, influencing everything from fashion to finance. There's data that tells us that social networks may be encouraging many people, particularly younger ones, to get involved in politics.[2]And there are few who would deny that the Obama campaign's ability to harness the Internet, social news and blog sites was a factor in his election. As Americans, we expect to pay attention to social media. But other nations are not far behind.

A twenty-two-nation survey from the Pew Global Attitudes Project in December 2010 found that, in regions around the world, people who use the Internet are using it for social networking. At least four in ten adults in Poland (43%), Britain (43%) and South Korea (40%) use such sites. And at least a third engages in social networking in France (36%), Spain (34%), Russia (33%) and Brazil (33 percent).[3]

Much of the new content available on the Internet is now being produced in Asia, with the largest community of bloggers in the world located in China and Japan.

The reach and power of social media has already been felt in global politics. In Iran's post-election riots of 2009, Twitter poked plenty of holes in the authority's media blackout, allowing Iranian cell phone users to update the world on events in their own streets and microbloggers from the U.S. and other countries to disseminate that information. Major news networks gleaned much of their own broadcast information from Twitter feeds and videos uploaded to YouTube. A friend of mine, along with many others, spent the entire day of June 13, 2009, relaying Twitter posts to guide injured Iranian election protestors to medical care and safe houses. Twitter even postponed a scheduled upgrade because of the prominent role it was having in Iran.

We saw a similar phenomenon in the Orange Revolution in Ukraine, and most recently in the events of January 2011 in Tunisia. While Ben Ali's government put a lock on traditional media, as well as on numerous national and international news sites, it failed to effectively censor social media. This gave protesters the ability to use blogs, Facebook, Twitter, Wiki documents, YouTube, and other methods to mobilize themselves and report what was going on. The very recent events in Egypt and throughout the Middle East provide other examples of the role that social media is likely to play in organizing and giving voice to populist protests in the future.

It may be inaccurate or premature to call any of these events, as some have, "Twitter Revolutions." But the fact remains that social networking played a large role, and we can expect it to continue to shape global events. Former UK Prime Minister Gordon Brown thinks that the Internet has "democratized communication," and has even gone so far as to suggest that Web-based social networking might have prevented the Rwandan genocide.[4]

I think there's cause for hope in that remark. And I, for one, have no doubts about social media's ability to focus opinion and sympathy. We've already seen the social Web mobilize millions worldwide for disaster relief and charitable giving. The Red Cross charity text message campaign after the 2010 earthquake in Haiti raised more than $10 million for victim relief.[5] The nonprofit organization Charity: Water.org raised more than $250,000 during only one brief Twitter-oriented campaign, and has brought in more than $20 million for Haiti using social media alone.[6] Technology made it possible, but social media got the word out.

None of this is meant to say that social media specifically, or even the Internet generally, has completely displaced traditional media. Not yet. But there's a fox in the hen house and the chickens are squawking. The pace at which social media is overtaking or altering traditional media is also phenomenal.

As traditional sources become weakened—or close their doors—in the face of a growing public preference for online information, many of the traditional outlets have little choice but to acknowledge and incorporate social media communications into their own. Print newspapers and magazines now discuss popular blogs and celebrity bloggers and post lists of this week's favorite websites. Headline TV broadcasters now feature their own "Twitter of the Day" or reach out to viewers to offer opinions on their own blogs and websites. CNN has made reporting of real-time commentary a regular feature of its daily news programming. The most popular element of an entire string of talent and variety shows is viewers' ability to vote interactively on contestants. The next day those viewers will chat about their favorites in their own online networks, which link to other networks, and the *New York Times*, and our local papers, will likely take note of all the chatter in their print and online editions. So it goes. An almost endless back and forth of reference and cross-reference.

The lines between digital media and traditional media are blurring. It's my belief that in a very few years that line will be nearly invisible. While I'm not sure how far traditional media will eventually be pushed down, or off, the continuum, I'm quite certain that the Internet will become increasingly central to a total media universe in which social media is the main ecosystem. The chatter matters. It matters to each of us already, whether we participate or not, and even if we are among that dwindling few who are not yet digitally connected. At this very moment, social media is improving the customer support you may need next week. It's damaging, or enhancing, the reputations of brands and products you use today. It's influencing prices, political opinion, trends in fashion, travel, entertainment, and much more in the world we all live in. Right now. And right now it's picking winners and losers in competitions we're not even aware of.

Social media doesn't stop at Facebook, and it's not a province only for the young. It has real-world impact on every individual, and on every industry. The challenge for business is not merely to acknowledge this importance, which is fundamental. It's not merely to become an active participant in the conversation, which is critical. The challenge is to master the total media ecosystem and use it to best position their brands in this new world of free discourse and connected consumers.

Conclusion

My goal in this chapter has been to run a brief panorama of the profound impact that social media has already made in the world and to provide a glimpse of which way the wind is blowing in terms of the future. I've tried also to highlight the interconnectedness of the information flow today—a flow that social media enables and energizes.

If you still think that social media is only Facebook, I haven't done my job. If you still think social media is merely a passing trend, I probably won't be able to get you to join the choir. But before you quit reading, I'd like to pose what I hope is a rhetorical question.

If social media can put a dent in your stock portfolio, influence who sits in the White House, disrupt global politics, focus the sympathies of millions in hours or days, or make a star of your ten-year-old virtually overnight, how can it possibly *not* affect your business?

Chapter 3. A Look at the Landscape

While we tend to think of social media, and often of anything digital, as being a "new" development, the facts don't really support that impression. Online social interaction has been occurring since the very beginning of the Internet, even preceding the dawn of the World Wide Web.

The origin of message boards, of user-generated content, even of online gaming, can be traced all the way back to 1979, when Ward Christensen developed the first electronic bulletin board. These earliest bulletin board systems (BBSes) were accessed over a phone line using a modem. Because users who didn't want to pay long-distance charges were limited to their own calling areas, the early BBS groups tended to be local. They did, however, promote true social interaction.

Online introductions often led to real-world meetings where users connected face-to-face. To a great degree, these BBS groups from more than three decades ago were the precursors to social networking as we know it today.

Even the practice of "tweeting," or delivering updates of one's real-time activity or status, has been around for more than twenty years, since 1988, when Internet Relay Chat (IRC) was developed by Finnish grad student Jarkko Oikarinen. Using a system of hash tags and @ signs, participants who were logged in directly or over the network to the same computer could ask for others currently on the system and then exchange real-time messages with any of those users.

And IRC had a global reach long before Twitter. It was notably used during a media blackout to break the news of the Soviet coup attempt in 1991 and to keep users current on developments in the first Gulf War. Many people stayed logged into IRC almost around the clock, employing it to pass on files and links and to keep in touch with their global network, very much as Twitter is used today.

With the advent of the World Wide Web, corporate Internet service providers (ISPs) began making inroads into bringing social, interactive experiences to the general public. CompuServe was first to inaugurate chat programs into a commercial service. Prodigy's contribution was significant in bringing down the price of ISP subscriptions. America Online followed suit, with massive advertising campaigns that lured millions more onto the Internet. In the 1998 film *You've Got Mail*, starring Tom Hanks and Meg Ryan, AOL went mainstream and we all learned just how social the Internet could really be.

The first website truly dedicated to social networking, however, didn't appear until 1997. It was called SixDegrees, based on a concept originally presented by Frigyes Karinthy and popularized in a play by John Guare. The idea was that a mere six steps—your friend of a friend of a friend, etc.—separated each person on the planet from anybody else.

The SixDegrees site encouraged users to create their personal profiles, to connect with friends, to develop new relationships, and to share information rapidly and on a sustained basis. SixDegrees was followed by Friendster in 2002, which was followed by MySpace in 2003, which was followed by Facebook in 2004.[7]

The history of social media is a fascinating subject, but its future is the relevant concern. What's "new" about the social media phenomenon is the speed at which it has lately become a part of mainstream culture and, for our purposes here, the value that businesses are finally discovering in relationship marketing. I'm not a social psychologist, but it doesn't seem like coincidence to me that social media is exploding as more and more commercial and government processes are being managed by machines, talking to machines. We're happy not to have to stand in line at the DMV anymore. We enjoy the convenience of doing our shopping on our cell phones or of getting our formal educations in pajamas at our laptops. But we're still social animals. And we like to stay connected to one another.

We're connecting today in lots of new ways. Entrepreneur and avid blogger Dave Harkins has theorized that there are generational preferences in the modes and methods we choose. Millennials, he thinks, who grew up in "expansive neighborhoods with overprotective parents" had no choice but to embrace social media—all of it—as a means of extending their friendships. His observations of Gen Xers, who were mostly in college when cell phones became affordable, suggest that they rely heaviest on cell phones for social interaction. Baby Boomers, however, while they may be comfortable with cell phones and email, function best in face-to-face interaction. This may explain why the Boomers are so quickly adopting Facebook, where they can "see" friends and connect with them through primary interests of hobbies, religious, or political views.

Whether or not there's hard science below Harkins's theories, he's definitely correct about the fundamental need to connect. Our styles and methods may be changing. Today we email instead of writing a letter. We text instead of calling. We share snapshots of the grandchildren by sending hypertext links to digital scrapbooks. But the deep need for social interaction remains. We need social media tools, says Harkins,

> "to help us maintain our ability to be human in the face of the demands made on us by our culture, our peers, and ourselves. These tools are now such an essential part of how we function as individuals and who we are together as a community, that living without social media and supporting technologies is unthinkable."[8]

For me, anyway, it seems equally unthinkable that these tools will not become an essential part of how businesses function. At the risk of stating the obvious, profitability in any business depends on people. However much we surrender to transacting with corporate automatons, or their software, we would all really rather deal with people. And we'd rather communicate in human than in corporate or institutional terms.

Social media helps to offset the depersonalization and anonymity of the digital world. It can help to define relationships, build trust, put human beings behind the brands and services, and generally work to de-commodify the buying process. Failure to humanize our businesses could lead to failure of our businesses.

For new entrants especially, the social media landscape can be confusing. But it's not the time to take a wait-and-see attitude. Tom Hayes, the author of *Jump Point: How Network Culture is Revolutionizing Business*, has written extensively about the need for businesses to regroup and rethink the future. He is not optimistic about those who don't. As Hayes puts it, "The freeway to the future is littered with the business cards of the blind-sided."[9] Delay is not the answer.

The Big Players in Social Media

In the discussion that follows, I am going to present a brief survey of the major social media platforms, or applications, as they look at the time of this writing. My survey is by no means exhaustive. It would take another book, perhaps several, to do that. But this review will provide a high-level description of the big players and give a sampling of the types and varieties of social media channels that are influencing your market—everyone's market—right now.

Facebook

Type:	Social utility
Method of Interaction:	Adding friends, posting photos and Web links, commenting on profiles, joining groups, social gaming
Main Demographic:	25–45
Number of Users:	About 650 million
Similar to:	MySpace, Hi5, Friendster
Business Value:	Brand building, advertising and public relations, extending sphere of influence, reputation management, lead generation

While Facebook was designed for and originally appealed mostly to the college crowd, its user demographics are currently undergoing a significant shift. Between 2009 and 2010, the fastest-growing age group became those over the age of fifty-five, an increase of 923 percent.[10] The growth, as well as the changing demographics, opens up a wealth of opportunities for business.

The migration to Facebook is occurring for several reasons. Many of these have to do with the site's technological innovation and adaptations. Facebook has made available a variety of intelligent and useful applications apart from the user interface and a range of mobile apps now integrate with the platform. Since social plug-ins were launched in April 2010, an average of 10,000 new websites integrate with Facebook every day.

Advertising on Facebook is not only economical but it allows for easy and very specific behavioral target marketing—a strength of social media marketing generally. Those targeted can extend well beyond your community of "friends" into markets as narrow, or as wide, as you want to make them.

Again, Facebook is not the last word in social media, but it's very hard to overestimate its scope and impact. If Facebook were a country, it would be the third most populated on Earth. More than half of the Fortune 500 companies already have a Facebook page. Any serious social media strategy must take Facebook into account.

MySpace

Type:	Social utility
Method of Interaction:	Adding friends, posting photos, commenting on profiles, joining groups, social gaming, music discovery

Main Demographic:	15–25
Number of Users:	About 60 million
Similar to:	Facebook, Hi5, Friendster
Business Value:	Advertising and public relations, extending sphere of influence, reputation management, competitive intelligence, musical exposure

Once the undisputed king of social networking sites, MySpace's popularity is waning and its traffic has declined steadily since August 2007. (It was overtaken by Facebook in May 2009.) But it may be too soon to count MySpace out. It is still among the top general-interest social utility apps and a useful advertising platform for music and other products with particular appeal to younger buyers. But MySpace's numbers are going in the wrong direction and its future is uncertain.

The story of MySpace's fall from grace contains an important lesson for businesses, particularly those just embarking on a social media initiative. The social media landscape is not static. Things change, and they change fast. Today's favorite platform could well be tomorrow's not-so-favorite. Even now, someone in a garage, a corporate incubator, or another of America's college dorm rooms may be developing the application that will one day eclipse Facebook. The applications and the platforms are certainly important, but they are far less important than a strategy that is able to stay on top of the changing landscape and is agile enough to make the adjustments.

Twitter

Type:	Social utility, microblog
Method of Interaction:	140-character comment exchange, referential interaction by relaying commentary ("retweets")
Main Demographic:	26–34
Number of Users:	110 million
Similar to:	Tumblr, Jaiku, identi.ca
Business Value:	Brand building, customer service and support, advertising and public relations, extending sphere of influence

The first-ever Pew Research Center study devoted exclusively to Twitter found that 8% of Internet users post a wide variety of content to Twitter every day with one-quarter of these checking in multiple times a day. Twitter also appears to be a good platform for reaching young minorities and urbanities, who lead in the demographics. Women and the college-educated are slightly more likely than average to use the service.[11]

The use of Twitter among the nation's largest corporations has nearly doubled: 60% of companies listed on the 2010 *Fortune* 500 have a corporate Twitter account with at least one tweet issued in the previous 30 days—up from 35% who did so a year earlier.[12] Mobile technologies are largely responsible for Twitter's growth. There are currently iPhone and Android versions, but desktop applications like Tweetdeck (for Windows) and Tweetie (for Mac) are widely used. A recent revamp of the Twitter application, which allows users to see pictures and videos without leaving Twitter itself, is likely to drive growth.

While it is possible to build a large following very quickly on Twitter, the key to successful tweeting is building an audience relevant to your company or brand so that you can quickly build trust and authority within it.

LinkedIn

Type:	Social business-driven community
Method of Interaction:	Connecting with new colleagues, creating partnerships, reconnecting with former associates

Main Demographic: 25–44
Number of Users: 100 million
Business Value: Establishing business
                          connections, job hunting,
                          recruiting, lead generation

Founded in 2003, LinkedIn was one of the first mainstream social networks devoted completely to business. Originally used to post résumés and to interact through private messaging, LinkedIn has become an important resource for recruiting, building authority, and showcasing skills, for extending your network and strengthening relationships within your existing one, even for tapping into new markets.

LinkedIn is not a forum for mass messaging, or for purely personal interaction, but by creating a profile, by joining groups, and participating in relevant conversations, it can be a valuable tool for recruiting, business networking, and creating partnerships. I recently received a LinkedIn message from a gentleman in Hong Kong who was inquiring about our RollCall Business Conferencing Service. That one exchange validated my own participation and reminded me of LinkedIn's international reach.

YouTube

Type:	Image and video
Method of Interaction:	Photo, video sharing, commenting and reviewing
Main Demographic:	25–34
Number of Users:	3 billion views per day
Similar to:	Hulu, Vimeo, Viddler
Business Value:	Establishing thought leadership, extending sphere of influence, public relations, general education, internal training, reputation management

While video is a fairly recent Internet innovation, it has quickly become the fastest-growing online advertising format, predicted to increase by 48% annually and to reach $7 billion by 2012.[13] YouTube is currently the world's largest video-sharing community and the second-largest search engine.

Short videos can be uploaded for public or private viewing and streamed to users from YouTube's site by way of blogs and other websites. YouTube provides code that can be embedded in any website page to view a specific video. For smaller businesses with bandwidth and storage limitations, YouTube hosting can be an economical way to add video to company websites.

Merely uploading a corporate commercial on YouTube will probably not get you the kind of attention you want, but if the video has entertainment or educational value, there's lots of potential for putting faces and voices behind your brand. How-to videos are especially popular, and even videos of sales conferences or new product rollouts can be readily accepted by the community if they're more "infomercial" than flagrant corporate ad spot. Videos from seminars and conferences that our company has hosted have been of interest to others outside the company. They've brought visitors to our site and been a valuable springboard for making new connections and sharing ideas.

Delicious

Type:	Social bookmarking
Method of Interaction:	Voting and commenting on articles
Main Demographic:	35–44
Number of Users:	8.5 million unique visitors per month
Similar to:	StumbleUpon, Faves, Squidoo, Furl, Blinklist, Reddit
Business Value:	Website and brand promotion, campaign tracking, establishing thought

leadership

Social bookmarking is the process of storing, organizing, and sharing your favorite websites. Users share these favorites with their contacts or friends list, adding descriptions, votes, or classifying tags or labels. Delicious, like most social bookmarking services, provides Web feeds for their lists of bookmarks and tag-organized lists. These allow subscribers to become aware of new bookmarks as they are saved, shared, and tagged by other users, and to see which sites are currently most popular. For many people, bookmarking websites have an intrinsic advantage over relying on search engines and other bots to categorize and qualify content because of the implied quality in a site that someone has taken the time to select and promote.

Digg

Type:	Social news
Method of Interaction:	Voting and commenting on articles
Main Demographic:	35–44
Number of Users:	24 million unique visitors per month
Similar to:	Propeller, Reddit, Newsvine, Slashdot, Technorati, Yahoo!Buzz

Business Value: Website and brand
                             promotion, campaign
                             tracking, establishing thought
                             leadership

Social news sites are slightly different from standard social bookmarking sites in their focus on specific articles and blog posts rather than on websites. Social news sites also allow users to save Web articles that have relevance to their user communities, making them accessible from any computer. Users also have the ability to participate in the discussion by leaving comments on popular news items. In Digg's case, articles can be uploaded in seven categories, including technology, science, world and business, sports, videos, entertainment, and gaming. The source of these articles may be blog posts or mainstream news outlets like Reuters or the Associated Press. Digg community users then vote the stories up ("digg" it), or down ("bury" it). The application also integrates with Facebook, allowing users to share Digg articles on their own Facebook page.

Social news and social bookmarking sites enable users to "curate" or aggregate content from the Web to serve as a resource to customers or the community. Businesses frequently use this feature to gather customer testimonials, to track and organize reactions to advertising and publicity campaigns, or to establish that they are on top of industry news.

Wikipedia

Type:	Information, online encyclopedia
Method of Interaction:	Creating and editing articles and information
Main Demographic:	18–29
Number of Users:	1,300,000 contributors, almost 400 million unique visitors each month
Similar to:	Wikisource, Meatball, Everything2, Quora, MyWikiBiz
Business Value:	Brand building, establishing thought leadership, general education

Wikipedia is the most extensive and well-known example of what can be done with wiki software, which allows any user to create and edit Web page content using any browser. Wiki supports hyperlinks and has a simple text syntax for creating new pages and cross links between internal pages on the fly. Wikipedia is social not just because of its user-generated content, but because the frequent updates make it a news resource.

While Wikipedia has been criticized for favoring

consensus over credentials in its editorial process, and also because its content is weighted too heavily to popular culture, inclusion in Wikipedia has become a definite status symbol. Having a current, well-written page on Wikipedia for your business can bring in new prospects and help the positive influx of detailed information shared about your brand.

Niche Networks

This review has looked only at general-interest social media applications, but a multitude of special-interest social media networks also populate the Internet. Some of these are quite large and corral specific subsets of people with defined needs and interests for niche marketing opportunities. One example is Ping, the music-only social network that Apple is opening up to its 160 million existing iTunes users. Niche social news sites, particularly for business (Tipd'd, Earners Club, etc.) or technology (DZone, Hacker News, etc.) are proliferating, and a multitude of specialized wikis, cult networks, and foreign language sites for distribution of social content also abound on the Web. Obviously, the value of any social media site depends on your business model and objectives, but knowing your audience is key to matching a strategy to a community's mindset and interests.

Other Trends and Currents

The Blogosphere

No discussion of social media is complete without mentioning the 70 million plus individuals who publish blogs (weblogs) and collectively form the most enormous and interconnected sphere of influence on the planet.

Technorati, which has published an annual "State of the Blogosphere" report since 2004, noted several important trends in their October 2010 findings. As might be expected, they found that the lines between blogs, microblogs, and social networks are blurring, but survey results also show that respondents believe that in five years blogging will replace traditional media for news and entertainment. At least 40% of respondents also say that their trust in mainstream media is dropping. The information they trust increasingly comes from other bloggers.[14]

Critics of the blogosphere complain that it's already too big, offering little more than eddies of circling information. This may be a legitimate criticism. The WordPress platform alone hosts more than 15 million blogs, many of which are simply a re-posting of other blogs. But for companies willing to commit to sustained, original content, the business case for blogging is still very strong.

The personal nature of blog writing helps to humanize your brand and is clearly the best way to show the personality and passion of the people behind your logo. Blogs can be a dependable stream of fresh and accurate information about your company or services. They function as immediate feedback mechanisms and can be important first alerts to customer service issues and for generating product development ideas. They help to raise company awareness, build customer trust, and drive traffic to your website. Blogs have become the interactive business cards in the great digital fishbowl. Most businesses will want to be represented there.

Webinars

The webinar (short for *Web-based seminar*), is an ideal way for participants to view a presentation without the hassle or expense of traveling. Viewers watch the presentation through their Web browser. Webinars can be broadcast live or made available on-demand. Some webinars provide for simple feedback, such as audience questions. Web-based seminars are frequently used for product demonstrations, informational sessions, or lead generation.

A more interactive version, the Web conference, allows for collaboration and more in-depth presentations.

Group members may share control of applications and can ask questions and give feedback in real time. There are free models as well as paid models for webinar broadcasting.

Producing and promoting webinars has value for lead generation, for heightening brand awareness, for growing networks, and for driving search engine rankings.

Podcasting

Despite its etymology, podcasts don't demand an iPod, since content can be accessed by other forms of portable media players or any computer that can play media files. A simple and inexpensive method for getting your message out there, the process involves creating an audio or audio/video file, adding it to an RSS feed, and submitting it to any of a number of host sites that maintain podcast directories. Podcasting is a natural choice for delivering information in a program-driven series that shares a host or a common theme and can be a valuable tool for companies that struggle with consistent communication.

It's the sharing aspect that can make the podcast social. If podcasts are promoted through your own website, through networks like Facebook or Twitter, and opportunities exist for listeners and broadcasters to

interact, podcasts can generate a lot of conversation.
Search engines favor podcasts above written content on
websites, and podcasts frequently get mentioned in
company and industry blog posts. Podcasting integrates
very well with other social media and can be an effective
part of an overall strategy.

Social Gaming

With titles like "Farmville" and "Pet Society,"
some of these may sound like child's play, but social
gaming already generates billions in real, grown-up
money. Estimates are that 79 million people will play
social games in 2012, up from 47 million in 2009—and
that's just in the United States. That growing audience
will translate to revenues from direct payments, indirect
sources (such as users acquiring virtual currency by
opting into advertising and lead generation), and direct
advertising of more than $2.18 billion in 2012. The sale
of virtual goods alone (think glow-in-the-dark cows, or
fancy collars for your digital dog) was estimated at $3
billion for 2010.[15]

In-game advertising and game sponsorships are
gaining traction, but developers like Arkadium, Zynga,
and Playfish are specifically building games for
companies who want to drive traffic and expand their
online presence. Brands like AARP are proving that

social gaming cuts across demographic boundaries. After launch of their gaming portal in 2008, traffic shot up to an average of 4.5 million page views, an increase of 294%.[16]

Location-based Social Networks

Location-based social networks (LBSNs), or location-based media (LBMs) have their origins in Japan. The first networks were primarily dating sites, using cell tower triangulation to alert users to others in their geographic location for romantic possibilities.

With the adoption of smartphones, however, the commercial opportunities inherent in geotagged content have become obvious, while the principle remains the same. Users typically create a profile and add friends. The mobile device's GPS can then alert them to the nearby presence of other members or of businesses or attractions participating in the network. Users can comment or make recommendations on area food, entertainment, or shopping. Local businesses can also "notice" members in the neighborhood and reach out with discounts and deals.

Some LBSNs, like Yelp, Foursquare, and Gowalla, include gaming elements that lure users to specific locations or offers. Users collect "badges" and points for various activities like checking into various tagged venues or retailers. Foursquare, for example, offers a "Jobs" badge awarded for checking into three or more Apple Stores. Showing the badge in the store entitles its owner to exchange it for a free "iHoverboard."

The market for hyperlocal social advertising is still in its infancy, but it's expected to grow up fast. The location-based mobile segment is projected to jump to approximately $4.7 billion in 2014, a CAGR of 75.6%.[17]

Yelp, Foursquare, Gowalla, Brightkite, Loopt, GyPSii, CitySense, and Plazes are the current leaders in LBSN apps, but we can expect new players to enter the space quickly. BlackBerrys and 3G iPhones already support most of the top networks. Social media and mobile marketing are just beginning to converge, but all the signs point to a dramatic change in the landscape over the next few years. I'll address this exciting convergence as it applies to social shopping and group buying in detail in Chapter 5.

Conclusion

While it's important to have an understanding of today's platforms and players, the goal is to harness the individual strengths of the most relevant platforms for a coordinated, holistic social media strategy. The objective is to drive conversion while personalizing, and protecting, your brand and reputation.

It's very much like putting a band together. You begin with the commitment. (*Yes, this is something we definitely want to do*.) You proceed to a plan. (*An analysis of these platforms suggests they are the instruments that will give us the desired effect*.) You may have to conduct some auditions. You'll make a few mistakes in getting the mix just right. And, of course, there will have to be lots of practice. But in a surprisingly short time, you'll start to make music out of the noise. I'll describe how the process unfolds and provide some steps and best practices for putting your own band together ahead in Chapter 7.

Given the overwhelming evidence that consumers are changing the way they communicate, companies need to embrace this change now if they have not already done so. About twenty years ago, companies of all sizes were asking questions like, Why do I need a website? Who will go there? What do I put on it? Is this really a trend or just a fad? Those questions really do seem silly in today's world where the first thing most companies do is create their online presence and begin the work of keeping their site updated, informative, and interesting.

Ten years from now the question of whether or not to embrace social media will seem just as silly.

Chapter 4. Customer Support Goes Social

Issues surrounding customer support are what got me immersed in social media, and I've already shared some of our experiences at ILD. Since we undertook a comprehensive and authentic online approach to customer service, I've been amazed at the ability of social media to provide good information to customers, clear up misunderstandings, and simplify issue resolution—to generally send signals that we care about our customers.

Providing poor customer service has never been a good idea. Before the social media explosion, however, it was still possible for companies to take a calculated gamble with a few customer complaints, a little bad press, even small product defects. Many companies survived, even thrived, while ignoring customer support issues or handling them on the QT. That won't be happening anymore. Social media is completely revolutionizing the customer support process, putting literally millions of unpaid reps on a 24/7 hotline that can work for you or against you. In the future you just won't get to have any "small" problems.

Some businesses have already learned the big—and expensive—lessons that can come to those who minimize a small customer service issue. United Airlines is just one of them. In 2009, when United Airlines damaged musician Dave Carroll's guitar and the usual customer support options failed him, Dave fought back by posting his original song "United Breaks Guitars" on YouTube. While the company still failed to respond, attention grew. After 3.6 million views, the airline donated $3,000 to the Thelonious Monk Institute of Jazz, but the damage was done. Within four days of the video's posting, United Airlines' stock price fell 10 percent, costing stockholders about $180 million in value. (Dave's performance also made *Time Magazine*'s Top 10 Viral Videos of 2009.[18])

There are plenty of other examples of companies that have damaged their reputations and revenues by failing to appreciate the influence of social media channels. But there are also some examples of those who misused that influence. The new social networks place a high premium on authenticity. And they don't like being manipulated.

Keeping It Real

I'm not ready to predict that social media will be responsible for the next great ethical advance of our species, but I can't help believing that it's going to take a deep cut in the number of liars, cheaters, and swellheads among us. Erik Qualman's book, *Socialnomics*, contains a chapter titled "What happens in Vegas stays on YouTube." Qualman labels the first crop of social media users as "the glass house generation," and notes that more than one student has been kicked out of college or lost a job for being much too honest about his activities or thoughts on Facebook. As more parents and grandparents join their offspring in the social media spaces, we're all becoming more cautious about how much we reveal to the world. This preventative behavior, says Qualman, is somewhat of a drag, but a good thing on the whole. It's making us adhere to the old adage, "live your life as if your mother is watching."[19]

It's not just individuals, though, who need to operate as if mom were watching. Social media communities are proving remarkably good at discovering, and punishing, companies who lie, cheat, or exaggerate needlessly.

In 2007 the CEO of Whole Foods, John Mackey, was found to have engaged in anonymous posting about his own company's stock and that of a competitor that Whole Foods was trying to acquire. He frequently disparaged the competitor's stock in an apparent attempt to weaken the value and improve Whole Foods's bargaining position for the acquisition. The respected executive had his reputation tarnished, was forced to issue a public apology, and endured investigation by both the SEC and an internal committee within his own company. Ultimately, no charges were filed, but this embarrassing episode overshadowed Whole Foods news for a year.[20]

Walmart suffered similar embarrassment in the fall of 2006. The blog *Wal-marting Across America* was supposedly being written by two regular folks who were taking an RV trip across the United States and stopping at Walmarts to visit with customers and employees. When Jim and Laura Rivers's RV trip turned out to be an ad agency contrivance, fans felt betrayed and the Walmart brand took the hit.[21]

There's plenty of pressure on companies these days to play it straight with consumers and partners, but many of them are discovering that the new premium on authenticity doesn't have to be a burden. Doing business as though your mom were watching may just turn out to be a better way of doing business. Those companies who are standouts in customer service are also perennial growth stories. It's no coincidence that most of these rely heavily on social media as an integral part of their customer support strategy or that transparency is key to that strategy.

There's no better example of this than online shoe retailer Zappos.com. The first-place winner for 2010's National Retail Federation's Customer Choice Award (and a top ten winner since 2007), Zappos is conspicuous both for the extent to which it integrates social media into customer service and for the value it places on keeping it real with customers.

Zappos has a blog team, even a blog bus. It has more than four hundred thousand followers on Twitter, which it employs in its call center operation. A 342-person, round-the-clock customer loyalty team answers 5,000 calls a day, 1,200 emails a week, and monitors Twitter and other social networking sites for mentions of Zappos, which they use to proactively reach out to potential shoppers. Zappos doesn't track call times or require operators to read from scripts.

When asked in an *Adweek* interview why the Zappos approach has resonated so well, CEO Tony Hsieh had this to say:

I think part of it is we're very transparent. One of our core values is being open and honest. It ends up creating more trust with our customers, employees, and partners. It's the opposite of what most businesses do. Most try to be secret with their secret strategies.[22]

Another young company that is learning the value of transparency is the Wi-Fi network, Boingo, a finalist in this year's Mashable Awards for Best Social Media Customer Service. Boingo connects to its customers on Facebook, Twitter, Flickr, and LinkedIn, and they proactively scan the Internet for comments and conversations that present an opportunity to jump in and help.

In an interview with Mashable, Boingo's PR and social media manager, Baochi Nguyen, noted that this proactive responsiveness is central to the company's approach to customer care. But the other thing that sets Boingo apart is a commitment to authenticity. "We don't hide behind our brand," says Nguyen. "We use our real names, give our real email addresses, and encourage our employees to engage with customers in ways that feel true to them and their style."[23]

This willingness to live in a glass house is becoming an important element of successful customer service strategies. Mckenzie Eakin is the Sky Captain of

Microsoft's Elite Tweet Fleet that supports their Xbox products. (The team, incidentally, is the most responsive brand on Twitter, according to Guinness World Records.) "We keep almost all of our tweets public," says Eakin. "We want our dirty laundry out there because we don't want to have any dirty laundry. That's a key accountability piece."[24]

Not every business will be willing to make this extraordinary commitment to openness and authenticity, and in some areas you probably shouldn't. For billing issues, for example, you don't want to respond on a public feed. But social media users expect honesty and authenticity from the brand and from those who represent it. The future of many businesses may depend on their ability to strip off the veneer of old marketing tactics and to move into the new glass house.

Making the Case

Make no mistake about it. Today's social media-savvy customers don't like being deceived. They expect honesty and reasonable responsiveness in regard to their customer service needs, and when they don't get it, they will take matters into their own hands. The downside of poor customer service is well documented on the Web. But there's an important upside to this new dynamic, too. Companies who foster a loyal community around their brands quickly find that customers will begin to answer one another's questions, to resolve issues or to validate complaints. ("No, you're not crazy. This is not an isolated case.") A customer community of mutual assistance can become an important first level of support for customer questions, resulting in cost savings.

For this reason alone I think that customer support may be the best place to build your business case for embarking on a social media initiative. Given that face-to-face interactions, followed by live calls, are the most costly means of addressing support issues, it just makes sense to avail yourself of the virtual army of unpaid, but willing, customer support volunteers. They're already hard at work for some companies who are getting a bargain from their efforts.

Here are just a few examples of companies whose social media initiatives are lowering customer service costs.

InfusionSoft

When this provider of marketing automation software decided to shift the focus of its community site to support issues, they got these results:

- The reduction of customer service agents to customers from a 1:55 ratio to a ratio of 1:172

- An increase in customer satisfaction ratings from 77% to87%

Cisco

Cisco needed a better way to organize product information and expert sources for account managers to handle customer issues. The company created the Specialist Optimization and Results (SOAR) initiative to bring its vast knowledge base together in one location. It provides access to virtual experts, discussion forums, and marketing materials. The company has seen these results from this initiative:

- Every 100 specialists can now do the work of 120, saving the company $5 million a year.
- Travel expenses for Cisco product specialists are down by as much as 60 percent in teams using SOAR tools.
- Specialists report that they are saving an average of 17 hours a week and boosting their productivity by 22%.

Pitney Bowes

Pitney Bowes employs a company-backed forum to provide customer service. While it constantly monitors the forum for customer issues, it waits a minimum of twenty-four hours before responding. This gives support staff time to properly research the problem, but it also provides an opportunity for customers to help out. Obviously, you need a strong community in place to make the latter feasible. Here's what PB gets from its forum:

- The company estimates that every 5 visits to a specific question on the forum or every 25 visits to a general post averts a customer service call.
- PB has averted a total of 30,000 calls to their customer service centers.
- At a cost of $10 per call, that means a total savings of $300,000.

According to PB's Mike Hardy, it didn't take long to start reaping these benefits. "While we don't generally share hard numbers about our performance," says Hardy, "I can say that we met all of our first year's expenses, including start-up, within six weeks of launching our forum."[25]

Another Line Blurring

Customer support is typically viewed as a cost center. Even when customer service and sales are combined, too many companies still fail to see the relationship between service and brand perception. They dismiss or undervalue the critical role that customer service plays in the big marketing picture. But the line between branding efforts and customer service efforts is blurring, if it's not disappearing entirely.

It seems to me that the businesses who don't get this have only a couple of choices. They can wait until some social media-driven PR disaster resulting from poor customer service takes a real bite out of brand image and earnings, or they can begin to integrate social media interactions into existing customer service, contact centers, and help desks, uncovering real cost savings while burnishing the brand.

On January 31, 2011, Jive Software announced the results of the largest customer survey ever conducted on the business impact of social business adoption. The responses from 500 individuals representing 300 companies worldwide reported these top customer engagement benefits:

- 42 percent more communication with customers
- 31 percent increase in customer retention
- 34 percent higher brand awareness
- 28 percent decrease in support call volume
- 34 percent more feedback and ideas from customers
- 27 percent increase in new customer sales[26]

An even more recent survey from Forrester found that nearly 5,000 consumers prefer better customer experiences even over lower prices. Another unexpected outcome of that study

> was the discovery that many of the obstacles that companies face when implementing change initiatives were resolved when the company deployed customer service social media initiatives. The key takeaway? Not only can companies transform customer service, but they can also successfully lead the changes required for better customer experiences—which drive business process improvements deeper into the organization.[27]

The hard data from studies like these, and the experiences of those companies who have changed the way they think about, and offer, customer service, demonstrate how pervasive the benefits of social media customer service actually are. The benefits also show up in better branding, new sales, better customer retention, even the ability to effect internal organizational change. The jury is coming back in. It seems that social media has value well beyond the intangibles of relationships or good will.

The Customer Has Friends

While I was in college, I had the good fortune to work for a great mentor in a high-end retail clothing store. While I was there I learned firsthand a great lesson in customer service. I had sold a sport coat to a gentleman who was very hard to fit. We tried several times with our head tailor to get the coat to fit to the customer's satisfaction, but after our third or fourth try, the customer became totally frustrated and walked out of the store in anger and frustration. I was stunned. I had never tried so hard to give a customer a satisfactory outcome and felt somewhat miffed that despite our best efforts, the customer lost confidence in us. As I mentioned, my boss was a great teacher and mentor who took the time to explain how sometimes trying hard and doing the right things will not guarantee that the customer will be happy. My boss said that the next time I encountered a similar situation I should just say, "We've tried our very best, but despite our efforts, it's not going to satisfy you. Why don't we try a different coat or let us give you your money back?" I was a little surprised by his comment because we really had bent over backward to make things right.

My boss explained that even though I may have been right, this customer might go back to his office and share his dissatisfaction with as many as 20 or 30 of his coworkers. I hadn't considered that aspect of the situation, but I learned a very valuable rule about customer service. Even though you may be dead right, it can potentially be harmful to attempt to prove it. Being right may not matter very much in certain situations. I was fortunate enough to learn this lesson at an early age. (You'll see more of this lesson highlighted in Chapter 6, which deals in depth with reputation management.) But if this was an important lesson then, it's even more powerful now. As Paul Gillin, author of *The New Influencers*, notes, "Conventional marketing wisdom long held that a dissatisfied customer tells ten people. In the new age of social media, he or she has the tools to tell ten million."[28]

Conclusion

While no amount of blogging, tweeting or Facebook interaction will replace traditional customer support, social media tools can certainly augment and enhance it, not just reducing costs, but fitting into larger marketing efforts. At a time when customers are becoming far less likely to call a contact center than to go online and vent to the world—and when negative information has an extraordinarily long shelf life—it just makes sense to extend customer service into real time where your customers are talking. Those companies who can take a proactive approach, reaching out with a helping hand into online chat, forums, blogs, and the social media networking sites where those conversations are taking place will be the biggest winners.

For the last few years we have tried our best to make ourselves a winner by making all of these initiatives a part of our company culture. It's just plain old smart business and our employees also appreciate our deep commitment to serving our customers. I've always preached that there is a direct correlation between trust and profit. If your customers trust and respect you, then I think you are likely to be profitable and stay around for a long time.

Despite all of your best efforts, 100% customer satisfaction may not be possible. But everyone in your organization needs to be highly committed to good customer service and to using social media as a major part of your customer service practices. The customer, remember, is *always* right. And he may have ten million friends.

Chapter 5. United We Buy: Social Commerce

Women, at least, have always understood the social component of shopping. As my wife and four daughters will gladly tell you, it's just more fun to shop together. They value the opinions of others when making purchases and feel more confident about their spending when a product or service comes recommended by someone who's actually used it.

Even we men—who don't necessarily turn the need for one item into a whole day at the mall—can appreciate this. We consult friends, too, when making purchases. If we haven't attended a Tupperware party, we might have been to a wine club gathering, and we've seen plenty of commercial advantage driven by social activity.

Regardless of our gender, and whether or not we'll admit to shopping just for fun, the Internet is making our shopping much more social. We're talking about our shopping. We're influencing each other's buying decisions. We're combining our purchasing power for more value and demanding discounts and deals. We're doing it in big numbers right now. Many experts predict that the group buying component of social shopping will exceed $3 billion this year. But we haven't even gotten started.

As a consumer myself, I find these developments tremendously exciting. But as an entrepreneur and a sales and marketing guy at heart, I can hardly control my enthusiasm. Social shopping creates huge opportunities for retailers and service providers. These opportunities can be national or local. They can be highly targeted via online communities and, if properly structured, can provide an immediate sales lift that can bring solid relationships as well as new customers.

Now that consumers of all varieties are perpetually connected by broadband and mobile devices, they can not only buy, but also influence purchases on a global scale, making social commerce a powerful and highly nuanced phenomenon that affects every industry. When you combine the "always on" consumer with the socially networked consumer, you have the elements of a profound transformational change in e-commerce dynamics. The data-driven, algorithmic marketing campaigns that have traditionally powered e-commerce in the Google marketplace are coming up short in the Facebook marketplace and in all of the other social networks where relationships and conversations now drive buying decisions. Rather than merely searching for dry information, consumers are increasingly seeking out the trusted referrals and recommendations of their friends and peers. Ratings, rankings, and reviews are now helping not only to humanize online commerce, but to put a lot of fun into it, and to prove, as the ladies always knew, that shopping can be very social indeed.

Ratings, Rankings, and Reviews

The late, great newspaper columnist and humorist Lewis Grizzard used to have a very funny comedy bit about the regional subtleties in the pronunciation of the word *naked*. Grizzard explained that, while most of the world pronounced the word *nā-ked*, many Southerners pronounced it *nekkid*. (Or as Grizzard said, "*ne*-double *k*-by God-*i-d*.") When pronounced *nā-ked*, the meaning was obvious—no clothes on. When pronounced *nekkid*, this meant that you not only had no clothes on, but you were more than likely doing something a little naughty as well.

Given the broad reach of the Internet, many businesses, sooner or later, are going to get caught a little "nekkid". While that exposure might be a little embarrassing, and in the short term might even cost you a sale, in the long term, it doesn't have to hurt your business. On the contrary, the willingness to move into the new glass house, to expose your "nekkidness" to the whole online world, could be the best business decision you've ever made.

I experienced my own illustration of this dynamic quite recently. I was doing a little online shopping for a pair of walking shoes on the website of one of my favorite retailers. The shoes appeared to be exactly what I wanted—the right size, the right color, the right style. Just before adding them to the shopping cart, however, I noticed that there were several customer reviews listed and decided to see what they said. I was glad I did. Unfortunately, for the retailer, the reviews were rather critical of how the shoes were sized and how uncomfortable they tended to be. I passed on the purchase, but my relationship with the retailer remained good, for two reasons: First, because I'd purchased from them before and had never been disappointed with their products, and second, they were willing to put forth comments from their customers even though those comments did not reflect well on that particular item.

I understand that no vendor can bat 1000, and I remain a loyal customer.

Almost everyone has had an experience similar to mine. Whether we shop online or in a brick-and-mortar store, our purchases are increasingly influenced by online ratings and rankings. This phenomenon represents an important shift in power to the consumer and can have a positive influence on your business—even, as in my example, when the rating is less than favorable. There are plenty of sound business reasons for incorporating rankings, ratings, and reviews into your website or elsewhere.

The most profound one is simply that customers trust them. In fact, 92.7% of shoppers have more confidence in information sought online versus anything from a sales clerk or other source.[29] By extension, customers also have more trust in companies that employ ratings and reviews—even when those companies occasionally get caught nekkid. For evidence, we need look no further than Amazon.com, one of the premier examples of how to effectively use rankings and ratings, a perennial winner of awards for best customer service, and, of course, an enormously profitable organization.

The user-generated content (UGC) that makes up rankings, ratings, and reviews also has a positive impact on traditional search engine optimization and the frequency at which your brand gets noticed. Search engines love fresh content. Because the UGC of ratings and rankings is usually in a fluid state, constantly being added to and updated, a Web page packed with your product names and related keywords makes great spider food.

Current information also resonates well with those seeking peer contributions (the wisdom of the crowd) and provides companies with a valuable form of market research through the discovery of newly emerging thoughts or trends. Online ratings, rankings, and reviews can play a major role in brand recognition, performance, and advocacy.

Social Shopping

Social shopping generally refers to an e-commerce addition that brings group members or shopping communities of like-minded interests to interact with sites that offer deals through group shopping sites. The common theme of social shopping is group buying at wholesale or discounted prices.

While most social shopping networks attempt to appeal to a broad base of users, there are a number of members-only sites that attempt to serve an exclusive clientele. Private communities such as A Small World, an invitation-only social network catering to the global elite, can drive a tremendous amount of commerce based on reviews, community connections, and highly targeted advertising. Gilt Groupe is the invitation-only shopping network that introduced flash sales to e-commerce by bringing the typical New York City sample sale into the broadband marketplace. Gilt Groupe expects 2011 revenues to hit $500 million. A similar "flash sale" site, HauteLook, was recently acquired by Nordstrom for $180 million in stock.[30] Mercedes, Starbucks, PepsiCo, and dozens of others also use private or branded networks for product development, market research, and brand advocacy.

In the following section, I'll provide a brief overview of some of the established and emerging companies that are offering new and exciting opportunities for merchants of all sizes. While many readers may be somewhat familiar with the sites and platforms contained in this overview, my hope is that even the most knowledgeable reader will still find some new and useful information.

Groupon

Started in 2008, Groupon claims to be the fastest-growing company ever. In December 2010 it turned down a $6 billion offer from Google. The company has achieved this meteoric rise by focusing on its primary revenue model—ultra-discounted coupons for local businesses, restaurants, salons, tourist attractions, etc. Occasionally the company will feature a national offering, like 2010's famous Gap coupon.

Groupon typically splits the proceeds from the sale of the online coupon 50–50 with the merchant. The merchant is solely responsible for honoring the face value price of the deal.

There is little doubt that Groupon is the 800-pound gorilla in the world of social shopping. The company has raised an estimated $25 billion in capital and has used their merchants to quickly expand their offerings into more than 150 US cities and 100 markets in Europe, Asia, and South America.

Groupon is one of the great business stories of our new century and its success has helped to spawn hundreds of new competitors. The following discussion features some of the most prominent of these.

LivingSocial

Considered by many to be Groupon's closest competition, LivingSocial has raised more than $583 million from Amazon.com and is projected to record well over $500 million in revenue in 2011. LivingSocial is another city-oriented deal-of-the-day site currently operating in 250 markets in 12 countries.

Dubbed a local activity discovery engine, LivingSocial enables people to find out what shops, restaurants, activities, and services are popular in their area, and offers new promotions every morning via its website, Twitter, Facebook, and an iPhone application. The company says it has dedicated "city experts" on the ground in every market, constantly researching the best in local attractions to bring a savings of up to 90% for consumers. Deals are live for 24 hours, as is typical for group buying sites, but LivingSocial also has an interesting referral model in place that helps to spur growth by giving users their deal free if they refer three friends who also participate.

While Groupon and LivingSocial are the independent group-buying giants, there are now services that will aggregate the daily deals in an area, grabbing info from Groupon, LivingSocial, and dozens of others. Two of these popular group-buying aggregators are Dealradar.com and UK-based Deal Romeo.

BuyWithMe.com

BuyWithMe.com is an online customer club that offers more than one deal per day and operates on a pay-per-performance revenue model. Local businesses and retailers promote specially discounted shopping deals to BuyWithMe's online membership with an important proviso. The deal will only go through if sufficient numbers of shoppers sign up for it within a limited time window. For each deal to become valid, there is a need to gather enough interested customers and meet the minimum benchmark before the deadline. This guarantees the retailers either status quo, or at least the minimum quantity of trade that will make their promotion profitable. The company is focused on allowing consumers to leverage group buying power to get large discounts with local merchants.

Woot!

The Woot! website describes itself as "an online store and community that focuses on selling cool stuff cheap." Companies offer deals on items like electronics, games, books, wine, toys, and more, one at a time starting at 12:00 p.m. CST, and continuing until the item sells out or is replaced by the next item at 11:59 p.m. CST. There really isn't any retail category that can be excluded from this site, making the possible deals extremely exciting. Another feature of Woot! is their flat-rate $5 shipping, which assures customers that there will be no hidden fees in any of their purchases. The company's marketing style is irreverent and often acknowledges its community of customers. Product descriptions commonly mock the product, the customer, or Woot! itself. Product drawbacks are preemptively acknowledged and buyers are advised to beware. An early pioneer in the world of social shopping, Woot! was acquired in late 2010 by Amazon for $110 million.

Blippy

Blippy is another site that allows people to publish information and start conversations about their everyday purchases. Blippy lets you communicate about and share purchases with friends by syncing to already existing e-commerce accounts such as iTunes, Netflix, Woot!, eBay, and more. Embedded access to the list of 250,000 retailers and restaurants allows users to get more specific about what exactly they bought. Thousands of people use Blippy each day to connect, converse, and comparison shop for goods and services.

Yelp

Considered by many to be the most popular review site in the world, Yelp has 50 million monthly readers of 17 million reviews in the United States, Canada, Ireland, and the United Kingdom. The business model here is ad revenue, coming from the mostly small companies that have received reviews. Yelp asks these to "claim" their Yelp page, which entitles them to traffic reports and allows them to respond to reviews. They are then encouraged to buy a sponsorship at $300 per month sponsorship that purchases advertising on the Yelp site.

While most of Yelp's reviews are positive, some are painfully, personally negative, and some business owners believe they have been unfairly damaged by a rating and review system they can't understand or control. "At its best," says *Inc. Magazine*, "Yelp is meritocratic, helping good businesses thrive. At its worst, Yelp empowers people who do not need to be empowered at the expense of those who are already struggling."[31] For better or worse, however, businesses in the 33 cities where it has gained a foothold are learning they can't ignore Yelp.

Foursquare

Foursquare is one of the location-based social networking websites available to users with GPS-enabled smart phones. While I mentioned the site in the Chapter 3 overview discussion of LBSNs, it's worth further development here for two reasons. The first is the site's phenomenal growth. Since its modest start in 2009, the service has grown internationally to 7.5 million registered users, up 3 million since the launch of Facebook Places. The second reason is that I personally know a real authority on Foursquare.

Angel Torres, one of our company's young IT stars, is my resident expert on Foursquare. I asked him to provide some background based on his experience. I think Angel's testimonial is a great illustration of how local businesses can generate loyalty for their locations and products and also for how much fun participants can have in the experience.

The following is Angel's response:

Mike,

I think of Foursquare as the most fun-to-use Geolocation app out there today. I call it "instant social gratification," since it also offers a very sleek gaming aspect, which allows users to earn hidden badges and become the "mayors" of a GeoPlace. I currently hold 27 Mayorships around town, which makes me feel special about those particular places. One of them is Target, where the manager, who is an avid user of Foursquare himself, always recognizes me. This happens again and again with places that I visit the most, and for the products I sponsor. My friends on Facebook and Twitter comment on the place where I am and the cool things to do there. (I just got a free espresso from Starbucks in Atlanta just by checking in and showing a code to the barista). It's that cool, instant social gratification again that makes this such a unique social environment to be a part of.

Group Buying: What Business Needs to Know

I know that many businesses are curious about social shopping and are attracted to the revenue possibilities in group buying. Many, however, still have fundamental questions about how the economic model works for the merchant offering discounted products and whether there's real value for lead generation and other business goals.

The Economic Model

The best and most detailed explanation of how the economic model for group buying works comes from our own Robert Ball. Robert posted this detailed explanation in a blog written for the *Huffington Post*.[32] Here's Robert's answer:

To develop a proper cost model for group buying, we must first remember that group buying is a form of lead generation and customer acquisition. Costs, therefore, should be captured, recorded, and, above all, measured as a marketing expense. Any conversations, therefore, must begin with a discussion of what your business typically spends to acquire a customer.

Second, you need to capture the *actual* cost of acquiring the next sale of a new customer, not a mythical if-I-had sold-that-much-at-retail cost. The way you do that is to base calculations on marginal cost and contribution margin: net sales revenue minus variable costs.

Let's use the example of Groupon's famous Gap deal from August 2010. As you may recall, Groupon ran a deal with the Gap: $25 for $50 off at Gap. According to published reports, 441,000 coupons sold for a total retail value of $22,050,000. Assuming that Groupon kept 50% of the coupon value, or $12.50 per coupon, then Gap received $5,512,500 in cash (441,000 x $12.50 – 50% of the coupon value). Based on the retail value of the deal, it "cost" Gap $16,537,500 ($22,050,000 - $5,512,500), assuming all coupons were used before expiring.

Now calculate the real cost: the marginal cost of those additional sales, taking into account only the direct variable costs, not other costs that Gap incurred anyway. That is, identify the costs that were incurred solely to satisfy the Groupon deal.

According to Gap's latest published annual financial statements, their 2009 costs of goods sold equals 59.7 percent. Their cost of goods sold includes such items as cost of merchandise, freight, production costs, insurance costs, and store rental. Gap's operating expenses average 27.5 percent of net sales, and that figure includes store payroll and benefits, marketing, design costs, merchandising costs and general and administrative costs.

Thus, of the 87.2 percent of the cost incurred per sale (cost of goods sold plus operating expenses), what portion is truly direct and variable? Assuming Gap did not add employees for the Groupon deal, then payroll and benefits should be taken out of the equation, as should freight (they only sold what was already in inventory), insurance, production and design. In fact, the only cost that should be included is the merchandise cost.

Estimating their merchandising costs are no more than a quarter of the costs—which is high—Gap's cost is not 87.2 percent of revenue, but 21.8 percent. Using that number, the marginal cost of the deal for Gap equals $4,806,900 ($22,050,000 x 21.8%), not $16,500 million. This is quite a difference, but still a loss. Or is it?

Let's look at a few factors I didn't consider. I did not take into account or assume any sort of "breakage" or that percentage of Groupon buyers who failed to redeem the coupon before expiration, which typically ranges from 10-20 percent. I also did not factor in the fact that a portion of those redeeming the coupon would buy more (or less) than the $50 coupon value, either of which would reduce the cost. I did not assume any repeat business that the Gap would get later from the coupon buyers—I presumed all were "one and done." And finally, I did not try to figure out new customers versus existing ones, or how many bought multiple coupons.

The combined effect of all of these factors would likely bring the cost close to $4 million. And if Groupon took less than 50%, the cost drops even further.

Thus, at my calculated cost of $4.8 million or so, the Groupon deal "cost" Gap around $10.90 per customer sale. I don't know if that's a little too high or a little too low. I do know that, according to *Advertising Age*, Gap ranked #80 in the Top 100 Leading National Advertisers for 2009 with a total U.S. advertising spend of $419.5 million. That's $1.149 million per day. On that basis, and not taking into account any of the other variables, the Groupon deal "cost" Gap what it would otherwise have spent on advertising over the course of just 4.18 days.

Looking at it another way, let's compare the costs to a typical ad budget of 10–12 percent of sales after taking into account cost mark-up. Assuming about a 90 percent mark-up for Gap, a 12 percent marketing spend to drive $22 million in sales would cost around $2.4 million. "A lot less than $4 million," you might say. Remember, however, that with traditional advertising, you pay up front and risk losing your money if the campaign doesn't work. In other words, would you rather pay $4 million after the fact for a guaranteed $22 million in sales, or $2.4 million up front, hoping to generate $22 million in revenue?

In the end, I come back to my admonition that you must structure the deal properly. If you do so and you use these calculations, you can come up with a group buying deal that eliminates upfront payments, assures the desired amount of revenue, and comes at an affordable cost. Now that's a breakthrough!

For some tips on proper structuring, I suggest you check out the recent study from Professor Utpal Dholakia of Rice University. It offers some ways to structure the deal that help lower the costs while ensuring a higher customer lifetime value. They include:

- Placing an upper limit on the number of coupons
- Rewarding "relational behaviors," like providing a coupon good for multiple visits
- Limiting the coupon to items that are high-margin or not as popular
- Limiting or restricting the usage of the coupon during popular times.[33]

As many have said, the success of group buying lies in customer retention and repeat sales beyond the coupon. That's usually the case with most any promotion. And after running the numbers, I remain firmly convinced that group buying deals, properly structured, are an excellent customer acquisition play.

On the issue of how group buying generates quality leads, I would like to turn again to Robert Ball. The excerpt that follows has been adapted from Robert's January 2011 *Huffington Post* column, "Group Buying Versus Traditional Lead Generation."[34]

Group Buying for Lead Generation

To determine how group buying weighs in as a lead generation tool, let's compare three popular lead generation techniques—free trials, paid lead generation, and rented/purchased email lists—to group buying in terms of cost, success in getting new customers, developing long-term value, and ability to measure results. The comparison reveals that, in many instances, group buying provides the superior value as a lead generation tool because of one key benefit: It produces a paying customer.

Free Trials

Free trials are everywhere, online and offline. You can't listen to the radio or browse a Web page for long without getting an ad for "15 days of online data backup for free" or a "30-day Try It Free" trial for Web meetings. Companies spend tens of thousands of dollars on banner ads, radio spots, site design, direct mail, and more just to give away their product or service, all for the prospect of converting a free user to a paid user. There's marketing costs, setup costs, and customer service costs all aimed at getting you to buy. And that's before you pay the sales team to contact the prospects and convert them to paying customers. Conversion rates vary, but 30–40 percent is considered excellent, so for the best programs you are only getting a new customer one out of every 2.5–3 tries, and that's after a heavy-duty selling effort.

With every deal, you get a paying customer, or at least a partially paying customer, so you start out ahead of the game. The buyer has paid something for the coupon, so you've already overcome at least part of the "perceived value" pitch, and if the buyer ends up being one-and-done, at least you got something for your efforts. You also didn't have any costs up front for advertising or selling, because Groupon or LivingSocial or OfficeArrow did that for you. Just try getting a popular talk radio host to pitch your service on a cost-per acquisition basis.

Paid Lead Generation

With paid lead generation, a common technique is to pay firms a fee for each lead they provide. It's up to you then to turn that lead into a customer. The typical price for a good lead can be anywhere from $30 to $50, or higher in some cases. Success depends on the accuracy of the lead information, how quickly the lead is followed up, how far into the buying process the lead is, etc. Success rates run from 20 to 50 percent at best. You pay for leads when you get them, not when—or if—the sale is made. As with free trials, leads typically require a sales team to make the calls and close the sale. It's a process that you hope will lead to a sale, but more often than not, it's just a hard out-of-pocket cost and a lot of effort.

A group buying deal matches the expense with a sale and a customer, and allows the sales force to concentrate on making the next sale to someone who is already an existing customer. Most say that it's five to seven times easier to make a sale to an existing customer, so you can do the math.

Purchased Email Lists

Lastly, you can purchase email lists at varying rates, and with widely varying success. I have seen marketing teams declare victory when an email campaign yields a one percent success rate! Thousands of dollars are spent sending emails to millions, hoping that a few hundred will become paying customers. There are the costs to purchase the list; the costs to send out the emails and deal with spam compliance and complaints; the costs to follow up and make the sales pitch, and, if all goes well, a close rate of one percent.

Group buying changes the dynamic completely because a group buying email list is comprised only of email addresses of those who have opted-in. This means that the person requested to receive the email that contains your offer. Group buying is sounding better and better, isn't it?

The questions for group buying are the same as for any lead program: Did I get a customer? Was it cost-effective? Can I measure it? Did I develop a long-term customer relationship economically? Measured against other popular lead generation methods, group buying holds its own quite well.

While group buying is not a panacea, I remain firmly convinced that it represents a breakthrough in lead generation and that it's here to stay, as it should be. The ultimate success rests with customer retention and repeat sales, but I like the odds that group buying provides—a paying customer for every dollar I spend.

Conclusion

I believe that social shopping is already changing e-commerce dynamics and the sales and marketing culture, and that it will provide opportunities for most businesses large and small. At our 2010 Lift Summit, there was plenty of excitement in the air about emerging B2B trends and about how wide open the space is for business-to-business group buying. OfficeArrow represents one option for companies that are interested in reaching a member community comprised of small business and office professionals. In our case, the deals are for office supplies, office products, software programs, and office devices, but the good news is that social shopping applications are all inclusive. Groupon practically covers the globe, but there are other local and hyperlocal distribution options that may serve you better, including those that use mobile phones to alert consumers to your offers. From the largest B2B enterprise to the one-location retail shop, promotions using social shopping applications are feasible for all businesses.

As with any part of your social media strategy, goal setting is all-important. Before you launch a social shopping initiative or campaign, you'll want to tailor your offering to achieve your desired results. Many companies can determine the cost of a promotion based upon their incremental cost of acquiring a new customer and find social shopping a cost-effective technique for new lead generation.

Another often-overlooked advantage of group selling is the opportunity to describe features and functionality in a product or service offering. And, of course, if you're willing to get a little "nekkid," those sites and programs that allow for real-time customer rankings and reviews offer powerful research and word-of-mouth-marketing opportunities for businesses big and small.

I don't know the ultimate outcome of the size and scope of social shopping, but I am confident in saying that its place will be a meaningful and permanent part of how most companies will sell and promote. As the number of companies in the social shopping space continues to expand, there will naturally be winners and losers. In addition to the established players there are many new entrants in the realm of social shopping. Slick Deals.com, Scout Mob, Kaboodle.com and, of course, OfficeArrow.com are only a few of them worth exploring. These new companies will continue to come up with innovative ways to create transactions both in B2C and in B2B, and as new applications emerge, they will complement existing ones. The mobile-only platforms are bound to proliferate, as will the location check-in apps for these platforms. But social shopping is a phenomenon whose time has definitely come. Already it can be a robust component of any company's social media culture and contribute to the ultimate goal of putting companies with customers at the customer's point of need.

Chapter 6. Reputation Management

Reputation is one of those "squishy" assets, hard to define and hard to quantify. As business owners and leaders, we recognize that reputation capital is as vital as any other type of capital, influencing a company's sales records, its stock valuation, its ability to attract quality talent, and much, much more. Yet strangely this valuable asset is not really ours at all. It exists out there, in an increasingly virtual world, in the aggregated perceptions of outsiders, who ultimately determine its value. In the theories of new economics, some have even called reputation a "hostage" in the hands of the organized consumer.

This feeling of being held hostage by an enormously large, interconnected army of "frenemies"— many of whom are not even our customers—can be daunting to traditional business leaders and seems to violate all we've been taught about business success. Suddenly it seems that producing a good product or service, running a sound business informed by good ethical practices, having a great public relations department, a strong customer service troop, even an phalanx of attorneys, just isn't enough anymore. The social media terrain feels like a landmine where, however carefully we tread, there's always the possibility of a misstep that could blow up our hard-earned reputation capital.

I sympathize fully with those who feel this anxiety. The social media terrain *is* risky. We assume some risk in merely having an online presence. But it's a moot risk, completely irrelevant if you hope also to reap the rewards of e-commerce. Fearing to tap into social media marketing is like being afraid to drive a car because you might get into an accident.

While there may never be any real consensus on exactly how one goes about assigning a dollar value to that squishy asset of reputation, there is increasing agreement for many companies that its value is being set by the conversations taking place in social media. In a very real sense, your reputation is in "their" hands. If you're doing anything at all online, they're talking about you out there. If you're doing most things right, the conversations are favorable. The fans are loyal to you and helpful to one another. They're working to build and burnish your brand and are bringing you new business, economically and commission-free. When you slip up and do something wrong—and you probably will, sooner or later—those conversations can turn ugly. They can hurt, a lot. And not just our egos, but the corporate bottom line.

Fortunately, there are ways to mitigate the damage, calm the waters, reassure the fans, and actually cement the relationships you're working to forge. Social media engagement is a risk management proposition just like any other. But for that proposition to pay off, we must first understand, accept, and fully absorb certain unpleasant realities of the online world as they affect our reputation capital.

The Brutal Truth

Our experiences at ILD taught all of us some basic truisms in regard to online reputation. These very simple facts would seem intuitive, yet they were hard won for us, and they have been for others. They're important enough that they probably should be on a placard on the desk of everyone who wants to get off the bench and into the game. These are the brutal realities of the online world, now made more stark in the wake of the social media revolution.

Bad News Travels Fast

That old expression "A lie can travel around the world quicker than the truth can get it shoes on" has never been truer than it is today. Reputations that have taken years to build can now be damaged or destroyed in minutes. Unlike the old word-of-mouth reputation damage, online reputation damage can spread like wildfire—the metaphor, which for good reason, is often used to describe the public relations disasters, like United Airlines' problems with Dave's broken guitar, that can become huge conflagrations almost overnight. Bad news travels fast. And the later it breaks—and the more sensational it is—the more likely it is to trump all the good news that came before it. Reputation should actually be the sum total of all your actions, but the most recent of those actions is by far the most important in forming opinions. Your reputation can be absolutely stellar, right up until the point when you do something a little naughty. An unfavorable comment shows up, sits unchallenged, and begins to garner links and reinforcement. After that, as the journalists say, "if it bleeds, it reads."

Brutal Truth: The sheer speed of today's Internet

means that any reputation management strategy must be nimble, ceaselessly vigilant, and turned on 24×7.

There's No Delete Button on the Internet

It's astonishing what a long shelf life the Internet provides to published information. For all practical purposes, it's there forever, sinking low enough, perhaps over time, to seem erased or irretrievable, but still there for those with the patience and persistence. It's very difficult, if not impossible, to get negative information removed or deleted.

Assuming that the damaging content is not infringing on your trademarks, violating copyright or the search engine's own anti-spam rules, you really have only three choices. You can sue, fight fire with fire, or ask nicely. Unfortunately, none of these approaches is likely to work very well.

Content removal lawsuits are very difficult to win. The First Amendment in the US Constitution guarantees all of us the right to express our opinions, however wrongheaded and fact-free those opinions may be. Webmasters have no liability for their forwarding links nor for comments posted by anonymous users. (That Anonymous guy, as you know, can be your reputation's worst enemy.) But more importantly, lawsuits frequently backfire. The negative coverage, new stories, and backlinks relating to a lawsuit usually do more harm than good, and legal proceedings often create official memorandum pages on government and court websites, which are among the highest-ranking pages on the Web.

The fighting-fire-with-fire approach fails for many of the same reasons. Counterattacking your defamer or employing Black Hat SEO tactics, like posting spammy links, invisible text, or fake consumer reviews, could result in a bigger problem than the one you started with. As we've already seen, the social media networks can be very forgiving over a little "nekkidness," but when they catch us masquerading, counterfeiting, or just being too darn belligerent or defensive, we're likely to be punished.

The third option for removing damaging information—that of asking nicely—is much more in line with the protocols of the new social Internet. Unfortunately, it, too, is a low-percentage play. Bloggers or message board owners may respond favorably to a request to set the story straight or remove damaging material or unfortunate links, if you can justify your position in detail, and if you do it reasonably and politely. The appeal of a phone call or message may be worth the effort, so I wouldn't completely rule out the "ask nicely" tactic for dealing with false information. But thinking that you can manage your reputation with this approach alone is a pure pipe dream.

    <u>Brutal Truth:</u> Effective reputation management campaigns must be proactive as well as reactive, incorporating positive content "push" strategies in addition to negative content "pull" strategies. There's no Delete button on the Internet, but the skillful use of SEO combined with social media marketing can make negative information much less visible.

You Can't Wait for a Problem

    This last brutal fact of reputation management is the most important. Reputation management through social media should not wait until you have a problem. At ILD, we did wait, and I'm here to tell you that we should have known better. Had we started a good monitoring and engagement program *before* those first brushfires, we might have saved plenty of time and money, and avoided a lot of stress. I've already shared some of the details of our own wake-up call, but far bigger companies than ours have also been caught sleeping, blissfully unaware that the new realities are about to take a bite out of their hard-earned reputation.

    You may have followed some of the travails of Swiss food giant Nestlé Corporation, which found itself in the eye of a social media storm last year. I'm including some of the Nestlé story here because it's a lesson-rich example for all of us.

The Nestlé Facebook War

In late March 2010 the Nestlé Corporation came under attack for the palm oil it was using in the manufacture of Kit Kat candy bars and other products. The palm oil came from an Indonesian company that environmentalists blamed for trashing Indonesian rainforests, threatening the livelihoods of local people, and pushing orangutans towards extinction. The environmental group Greenpeace launched an online protest, spurring a groundswell of criticism on Nestlé's Facebook fan page, creating anti-Nestlé advertising on YouTube, detailing its claims on Twitter, and issuing a voluminous report on how the company's practices threatened rainforests, contributed to global warming, and endangered the orangutan population. The attacks included the creation of an altered Kit Kat candy wrapper that replaced the brand label with the word "Killer" carried by an orangutan.

Nestlé's first mistake was in being caught off guard. They were obviously not monitoring their own brands well, and certainly not their potential vendors. If they had been, they would have seen the fire hazard, as this vendor had already been cited by Greenpeace and a lively conversation about the topic already existed on the Web.

The bigger mistake, however, was the tone that Nestlé took with its damage control approach. Nestlé responded defensively, emphatically telling Facebook users it would delete their comments from its fan page if they included the altered logo. This incensed the protesters and Nestlé's Facebook fan base increased dramatically to more than 95,000 fans, mostly made up now of decidedly unfriendly protesters.

Maybe Nestlé didn't know how well the user-generated content of social networking sites can rank. Or that an active social media account with your brand in the username can theoretically outrank your company's official site. But Nestlé's reputation had been taken hostage.

It's not totally clear if Greenpeace staged and executed the whole attack, but regardless, the community was relentlessly dog-piling on the brand's Facebook page. Nestlé did respond with a Q&A on its corporate site, but it essentially retreated from the Facebook discussions, leaving the page open for detractors. Hostage abandoned.

It's worth noting here that the amount of palm oil purchased by Nestlé from this particular company was only 1.25%of the total palm oil purchased. Nestlé might have chosen to fall on its sword, admitting *mea culpa* for the tiny fraction of offending palm oil, and thanking its fans and customers, even Greenpeace, for the enlightenment. It didn't. We can only imagine the true cost of that decision.

The facts, at any rate, might not have mattered to the folks behind the campaign to bring Nestlé to its knees. Indeed, the entire incident illustrates just how insignificant the facts can often be in a full-blown social media war and as they pertain to reputation management generally. It's not about facts. It's about perception. And Facebook users perceived Nestlé as hostile, defensive, and indifferent.

In the aftermath, I think that Nestlé Corporation learned a lot about the new realities of social media. They learned how fast bad news travels, paid the price for not paying attention, and found that we don't get to dictate the terms of engagement. Our reputation is in their hands—we're not the ones to make the demands. Finally, I believe that Nestlé discovered that underestimating, or turning your back on, the social media communities will not serve you well in protecting your reputation capital.

Nestle spokesperson Nina Backes said it for a lot of us in her assessment. "Like all companies," Backes said, "we are learning about how best to use social media, particularly with such complex issues. What we take out of this is that you have to engage."[35]

I think that Ms. Backes is correct. We do have to engage. The failure to engage is to forfeit all the incredibly exciting possibilities of the new social Web. But listening needs to come first.

Listening In on Social Media

Monitoring is the first step in obtaining a baseline of conversation. By baseline, I mean not only what is being said about you or your company, but where it is being said and how the conversations are being conducted.

There are a number of readily available social media monitoring (SMM) tools on the market today. None of them are perfect. In our own use and analysis of some of the available tools we saw a number of holes and thought we could do better—a key driver behind the development of Social Strategy1. From the beginning, however, we realized that technology alone wouldn't determine our success. In the next chapter, I'll describe the stages through which a successful social media strategy evolves, and you'll see why an effective strategy must precede the focus on technology.

What to Monitor

The key to making any SMM tool work

effectively both from a cost basis, as well as the use of your human resources, is choosing the proper search terms. Search terms are the basic terms used by the SMM tools to bring data back into the system. If your search terms are too broad, you'll get a ton of data that is not relevant, and if your terms are too narrow, you will miss conversations that may be meaningful. You may need to experiment a bit to refine your search terms in order to collect the most relevant data possible.

Obviously, you'll search for mentions of your company name and URL, but don't forget d/b/a names, sound-alikes, and the possibility that others may be attempting to capitalize on, confuse, or muddy your reputation. You'll search your product and brand names, product URLs, brand images and slogans, and certainly those of your competitors.

Depending on your type of business, it can also be valuable to monitor business partners, major clients or customers. Knowing about the achievements or positive news surrounding your customers will enable you to link back to that good press, thereby benefitting both of you.

It's also worth investigating the reputation status of your company principles and any public figures associated with your brand. You may also want to profit from Nestlé's lesson and search the reputation status of your vendors.

Where to Monitor

Once you begin listening to what consumers are saying about your brand, products, and competitors, you'll have a better sense of which platforms to monitor for certain types of feedback. If you already have a social media presence, you'll start there, of course, by monitoring the comments that your fans, followers or subscribers leave on your own social profiles. This is the first step to mastering your listening skills. Social search tools like Stumbleupon and Reddit, and social voting tools like Digg.com, and others mentioned in Chapter 3, can help with turning up commentary in other social networks.

As a secondary step, monitor buzz elsewhere. Use Twitter advanced search (or Twitter clients like Search.Twitter.com, Hootsuite, TweetDeck or CoTweet) to monitor key terms around your business, including your brand names, trademarks, product types and competitors. Use Google Alerts to keep up with the latest news about your company. Search comments relative to your domain and mentions of your brand in blog posts via Google Blog Search or Technorati. In addition to blogs and traditional news sources, discussion boards are another networking channel where conversations about you may be taking place. Don't forget to subscribe to relevant wiki pages so that you'll know when pages have been changed. Search image and video sites like YouTube, Flickr, and Slideshare. And you'll want to find out who's listening in on you, too. SEOPro or a similar tool can show you who is linking to your own website or blog.

Now I've already mentioned a number of tools. I've certainly omitted some. Some of these SMM apps, while inexpensive or free, are quite rudimentary or else quite specialized, doing a pretty good job at one small task. By the time that we go to press some of these tools may have been improved. Others may have already disappeared, having been replaced by something newer and sexier.

The selection, experimentation and coordination of all these tools can be challenging. At ILD, because we waited until we had a problem, we found the beginning of our monitoring process especially demanding. We were also launching a new customer resolution platform, establishing our own social presence, learning how to engage with consumers in an entirely new way, and improving our overall business processes.

While embarking on your own reputation management strategy, you, too, will have to continue to run your core business. There's a lot of juggling involved. I won't minimize the time, energy and resources that may be required and there's a good argument to be made for outsourcing reputation management. But the decision to outsource may wait until you've gotten your feet wet. Until you've discovered where the conversations are taking place, what damage you may need to repair, what customer service deficiencies turn up, and what opportunities you may be missing for lead generation. It's from the listening phase, though, that the goals and priorities of a comprehensive social media plan will emerge. The more you learn here, the better prepared you'll be to vet a solid provider who can incorporate reputation management into your primary business goals.

Regardless of what agency or consultant you ultimately hire, or what tools you may finally settle on, I strongly encourage those embarking on a social media strategy to undertake at least the beginning of the listening phase yourself. This is where the learning and the consciousness-raising takes place.

Reactive and Proactive Responses

Most companies don't concern themselves with reputation management until that first brush fire. Developing and implementing a reputation management plan then becomes a scramble. It may be that a good, sustainable plan can actually be developed this way, in the middle of all that smoke and heat, but it's surely not the best way.

Reactive Responses

Just as disaster plans are designed in the hope that they'll never be used, the reactive components of a reputation protection methodology can be in place before they're needed. The more specific you can make them, the more prepared you'll be. Knowing how to triage customer complaints is important, but the speed of the reaction is critical. Allowing questions or complaints to sit idle on a social network is like inviting ants to a picnic. Those companies who are serious about preserving their reputation capital invariably train internal experts to capture complaints in social networks and to solve issues in real-time on the channel of the customer's choice. Being able to react quickly to complaints is the best safeguard for your reputation. Being first on the scene for complaints about your competitors has its advantages, too.

One company working this advantage is 8th Continent Soy Milk. In a recent promotion, 8th Continent monitored mentions of Silk brand soy milk, a competitor, and offered trial coupons to users. In one instance, community manager Sarah Lopez picked up on consumer Weily Lang's tweet about a bad experience she'd had with Silk chocolate soy milk. Lopez jumped in with a coupon offer, which Lang thanked her for, and subsequently redeemed that week.

In an email interview with Mashable, Lopez reported, "with coupons distributed via social media, we've seen a 39% redemption rate, versus the 0.7% redemption of hard copy coupons. During coupon promotions we saw huge spikes in our fan base and a lot of pass along."[36]

I think the 8th Continent promotion is a great illustration of not only how good monitoring pays off, but how reputation management fits into the bigger marketing and branding picture.

Proactive Responses

Proactive responses include your "push" activity—the steps you will take to crowd out unfavorable publicity or negative reviews. Even as you're contemplating your first social media initiative, you can begin to beef up your online presence. Inventory your existing sites and other digital assets to determine if they're well optimized for your target brand or name keywords. If not, start filling in the gaps with optimized pages, and optimized title and meta elements. Link strategically to other relevant sites and use paid search or other tools to increase your visibility. Experiment with the SEO of your sites and observe what changes in terms of Google traffic vs. social search. Since most people don't usually look beyond the first pages when they use a search engine, you can control your online reputation by filling the top slots with content that presents your company positively.

The creation of new content is as fundamental to reputation management as it is to any other social media objective. Once you're directly engaging it's important that your blogs and fan pages are updated regularly with relevant, informative data and that your posts are being optimized properly for search engines. Optimizing your relevant posts and staying fresh and interesting can go a long way in influencing potential customers, vendors and even people who may initially want to complain.

Most importantly, avail yourself of all the tools and the spaces and places where your customers might be. I'm a big believer in video, for example, and find that its rising popularity is making it one of the most powerful in the reputation management toolkit. Having a relevant keyword-based video on YouTube, one that ranks on the first page of search engine results, can push bad reviews and negative comments to near irrelevance. To be most effective, the videos should be tagged with the relevant file name, keywords, placement and channel. Google and the other search engines change their search algorithms frequently, and SEO optimization is the subject of many other books, but currently there's almost nothing as valuable as video for outranking negative publicity.

While it may seem counterintuitive, the most truly proactive step that any company can take is simply to provide a place where its customers can complain. When you can direct commentary to your own site, you're better able to address the issues and the information sharing that takes place on such sites works to reduce complaints generally. I speak from some experience is saying that this is a far better solution than waiting for disgruntled customers to create their own blogs, and their own negative SEO.

The combination of these proactive and reactive approaches to dealing with negative publicity, along with constant monitoring, should keep those reputation brushfires from getting out of control.

Playing Nice in Social Media Engagement

An assault on your online reputation may come from many quarters. It shouldn't come from within. Yet many companies create self-inflicted wounds by failing to understand the very essence of social media. We all know that it's not just what we say, but *how* we say it. Taking the wrong tone, being hostile or too aggressive can be just as self-sabotaging online as it is in any human relationship. None of us wants ourselves, or our companies, perceived as bullying, selfish, dictatorial or insensitive. Here is my compiled list of some of the best tips and practices for avoiding that perception.

Listen

It sounds like I'm harping on this one, but it's vitally important. By listening, of course, I do mean monitoring what is being said about your brands and company. But I also mean listening for our own edification. It's really the only way to "get" social media and the only way to identify trends and opportunities. The whole planet is beginning to speak social media. That means that CEOs and C-level executives will need to be fluent in it in order to keep their companies relevant.

Participate, Don't Dictate

This is a struggle for many companies when they uncover negative, sometimes patently false, information in reviews, on message boards or on blogs. But if you try to dictate, take down or manipulate the conversation you will alienate your followers and do more harm than good. Respond with facts, but don't be defensive.

Provide Value

There's a lot of competition for ears and eyeballs

out there, and it's going to get worse. The best way to insure that you get a share of positive attention is by contributing something of value to the conversation. Simply recycling old blogs or creating a vacuous framework for links won't cut it. You need to give your users something useful, unique, interesting and engaging. Talk about what's important to your community. Solve a problem. Give away helpful information. Offer a discount or a deal. But give them something valuable and they'll keep coming back.

Share

Even though you've written and published content, and therefore own it, you'll have to relinquish some control so that it can be syndicated across the Internet. Allow others to share what you write. Similarly, you'll be expected to share the content of your own friends, partners, and influencers. Give back, reciprocate, and recognize notable contributions from participants in your communities. There's a definite, "scratch my back and I'll scratch yours" dynamic to social media.

Be Authentic

Social media is a less formal forum and there's lots of opportunity to lighten up a little. But your engagement and responses should still be consistent with your brand and message. Professionals like accountants or lawyers shouldn't try to affect the voice of an interactive gaming company just because this is social media. Your audience will see through it immediately and your reputation will suffer.

Be Reliable

Once you start to engage, be committed to it and consistent. Engaging only when you have a problem won't build relationships. If you have a blog, post to it regularly, ideally on the same day of the week, or the same time of day. Respond to questions and comments in a timely fashion so that users will know you're still on the job.

Be Honest

Responses that lack integrity or are simply not true will be particularly harmful. You must be completely, open, accurate and honest. Corporate bloggers should use their real names, identify the company they work for, and be clear about their role. Acknowledge problems where they exist, and talk about your solutions. People respect honesty.

Drop the Hard Sell

Don't use social media solely as a sales tool. Certainly you want customers to be aware of your product or service, understand its benefits, and have a way to purchase. But if your content is nothing but market hype, they'll lose interest in what you have to say.

Think Twice

Since there's no delete button on the Internet, what you say is going to be around for a long time. Make sure you're ethically and professionally confident about what you publish. Comply with corporate usage policies and be mindful of relevant confidentiality, copyright, and similar restrictions. If you choose to make remarks that are deliberately provocative, then be prepared for the skirmish.

Always Say "Thank You"

It sounds fundamental, because it is. Whether they're griping or singing your praises, acknowledge the time and attention that it's taken to comment.

Conclusion

While reputation may be hard to measure and define, we all know it's both valuable and vulnerable. Since it resides in the perception of outsiders, who now have the ability to broadcast their opinions indelibly and quickly, we have to be ceaselessly vigilant about guarding that reputation. While technology can help us create an early warning system for threats to our reputation capital, it's up to us then to act quickly and appropriately. Combining reactive (pull) techniques with proactive (push) approaches can go a long way toward ensuring that the online viewer sees us at our best. These same techniques, not at all coincidentally, can also uncover opportunities for new customer relationships and new business. Finally, our reputations are best served when we engage in ways that are respectful, ethical and honest.

Chapter 7. Social Media Strategy

The motives for deciding to participate in the social media ecosystem are as variable as the companies, and the people, that compose it. In the case of ILD, it was a reputation management issue. Your own motivations may be entirely different. There's no single best reason for embarking on the social media seas, no "one size fits all" template for planning the voyage, and once you get onboard you'll find no hard-and-fast rules.

From our own experience, however, as well as the experiences of those organizations we work with through Social Strategy1, we've discovered some definite phases, or stages, which most companies go through, and where specific stage-related learning and activities take place. The stages I'll describe here are ideal. They contain many of the ideas and best practices that were presented by thought leaders and innovators at our 2009 and 2010 Lift Summit conferences. In actual practice, these stages are rarely self-contained, tidy, and linear. They will overlap and involve some backing up and starting over. The process of learning about social media, and of applying that knowledge, is organic and highly iterative. But a successful strategy will evolve much like this and go through these general progressions.

The Listening Stage

The first phase of any social media strategy is the listening stage—the consciousness-raising stage, where you discover what they're saying about you, or not, and where those conversations, for good or bad, are taking place. I've described the listening stage and some of the monitoring tools that can be used in this process in detail in Chapter 6 on reputation management. The takeaway, I hope, from that chapter, is that the monitoring stage should be well orchestrated and comprehensive. You may have been listening before in the same way you read for pleasure or distraction. Now, however, you're reading for the big test. You're studying now, in an organized way and with a specific goal of knowing everything you possibly can related to the subject matter of your company. The listening stage should be approached with high seriousness, and you need to take terrific notes.

While the listening phase is the undisputed starting point for any social media strategy, it's important to say that the listening never stops. Once the cotton comes out of the ears, it stays out. Without ongoing monitoring and intelligence gathering, there simply isn't any way to inform a strategy or gauge its success.

The Planning Stage

As I discuss social media with other executives, I am often surprised that they have no social media plan at all or have a plan that is focused on relatively minor concerns or initiatives. Certainly, some goals will be short-term, quick-hit campaigns. Planning and execution for these initiatives is just as important as it is for ongoing strategic goals. But a campaign is not a strategy. I would like to see more companies approach social media with the same kind of comprehensive, tactical planning that they would use for any other major business initiative, expansion, or sweeping change. Many organizations, in fact, will find that social media is the biggest game-changer they've ever encountered. But even if, for now, you still view social media as just one more distribution channel for traditional marketing efforts, it's important to set clear goals and objectives.

Or, as I like to say, "Plan your work so you can work your plan."

Getting Management Buy-in

Now, I have a strong bias that a company's CEO should lead any company's social media initiative. The CEO should lead by incorporating his or her overall plan for the company's growth and development. If the CEO has determined that new products or brands should be launched, then certainly social media should complement these initiatives. If growth via acquisition is a strategic goal, then social media can be very valuable in searching for possible targets as well as being a meaningful part of due diligence efforts in evaluating any potential acquisition opportunities.

In the event that someone else will lead the effort, it's still critical that management is on board here. It may be necessary to distill what you've learned from your social media monitoring stage into an executive report or other communication. In our own case, we called a meeting to inform stakeholders of what we'd learned and to begin brainstorming ideas. Communications, of course, are always complicated relative to the size and structure of organizations, but some method must be found for providing decision makers with the information they'll need to understand and support the planning efforts.

The purpose of the planning stage is to determine what you want to get out of social media engagement. Do you need to humanize your image? Do you need forums for better, more cost-effective, customer resolution? Do you want to capitalize on social media opportunities for lead generation? For recruitment? To establish yourselves as industry experts? To tap into the mind of the crowd for product development? It's not a Chinese menu. You don't have to pick just two. But some priorities should emerge to inform your first steps. You may already be facing a messaging obstacle or, as in our case, a reputation management issue. These goals will naturally rise to priority status. All plans, of course, will change and adapt, but a roadmap will keep you from driving blind.

From our own meetings we created an initial plan that looked something like this:

- Develop an automated consumer resolution application to provide billed consumers with a tool to facilitate quick self-help and to alleviate pressure on the call center
- Create a community forum to enable consumers to vent and resolve billing issues within a controlled site

- Triage customer complaints (map out a plan for mitigating escalated complaints, resolving inquiries, routing consumers to resolution, etc.)
- Establish a social media presence (create profiles on Facebook, Twitter, LinkedIn, etc.) and start to bolster our Web presence with social media features
- Refine and organize our ongoing listening and monitoring process
- Develop a plan for managing future negative publicity
- Improve the company's first page search engine results (promoting a theme of advocacy and transparency)
- Improve our overall business processes relative to our social media efforts

As you can see, our plan was heavily prioritized toward customer service and there were obviously many small steps involved in each of the larger ones. Your own plan may look different. But a clear benefit of defining objectives in this way is that they can guide the timetable for implementation. It's natural, once the list of objectives is established, to want to implement everything and all at once. Natural, but not realistic. It took us approximately six months to fully execute our entire original plan, longer than we expected, but the consumer self-help site, which was a priority, was rolled out quickly, and we processed 15,000 inquiries in the first month alone.

Today our social media strategy planning—across three companies—has been expanded to include many opportunities we hadn't thought of then. These include several blogs, the creation of our own user communities, group buying initiatives, ongoing education and outreach programs through our Lift conferences, the webinars we distribute through YouTube channels, and more. But that first strategic plan for ILD served us well as a blueprint for goals that were manageable, realistic, and achievable.

Spreading the Word

Once you have your plan, and the management buy-in to make it happen, it's a valuable next step to shop it around internally. Communicating your goals company-wide will create your own internal buzz and empower your own people to make those goals their own. This is also the best way to discover hidden resources within the organization. You may already have, as we did, experienced bloggers, good writers, or evangelists for particular platforms whose talents can be important in the delegation of resources. In all likelihood, many in your organization are well ahead of management in their social media awareness. Whether they are active with friends and family on Facebook, networking with fellow professionals in groups like LinkedIn, or avid shoppers using rankings and ratings on social shopping sites, I'd wager that a majority of them are very involved. It would be a shame not to take advantage of their savvy and enthusiasm.

In our own organization, we have Chris Craven, one of the senior guys in our RollCall Business Conferencing division. Chris is a real social shopping mover and follows most of the named flash sales sites, while also checking on smaller sites and those that are aggregators of other deals. If you want to know whether something is really a good deal, just ask Chris. We also have an in-house Yelp expert, many avid Facebook users, and some experienced writers, bloggers, and researchers whose talents come in handy.

Our staff often comes up with creative ways to use their social media expertise. A few weeks before this year's Super Bowl, for example, our lead developer for our Social Strategy1 platform, Darren McDowell, asked about using the platform to monitor real-time and follow-up chatter for famous commercials. We told Darren to go for it and he was able to follow more than 400,000 mentions. We didn't monetize this effort, but from Darren's experiment, we developed valuable information that we put in a detailed white paper. I'm confident that this white paper will provide prospects with a very favorable picture of what our platform might do for their business.

So spread the word about your social media initiatives. And let all of your staff—not just the Gen Yers—know that their talents and creativity will be welcomed in your efforts.

The Initial Engagement Stage

In the initial engagement stage, you'll begin to establish your online presence. Here you'll create basic accounts and the profiles you'll be known by in the great conversation. There are obviously far too many social media platforms for any company to participate in all of them. Choose a few for the initial engagement stage—I'd definitely recommend Facebook, Twitter, and LinkedIn. Your plan may have determined that your initial focus area of engagement is the greater corporate image or you may instead choose to select an individual service or particular product in your brand line. The time may come when you'll have a great many social presences online, but that's no reason not to plan now for consistency in image and messaging.

Staying Consistent

I've seen a definite temptation by those new to social media, or new to a particular platform, to see this novelty as an opportunity to present a brand in a whole new way or from an entirely different angle. The lack of consistency, however, can be confusing to customers or contradict your real value proposition. I'm all in favor of experimentation with social media. And there's no denying that different sites demand different protocols for interaction. While you might need a little design tweaking so that graphics render properly on new blogs or social profiles, you don't need two different logos for Facebook and Twitter. Your image, voice, and values should be consistent across channels.

Committing to Content

It doesn't take very long at all after launching a social media strategy to realize that content is king. Early on you'll benefit from brainstorming for editorial content and creating an editorial calendar, especially if you're beginning a new blog. The initial engagement stage is a good place to inventory existing traditional content to see if it can be used on, or adapted to, social media sites. And, since the listening hasn't stopped, you'll likely be developing content based on what you're learning.

To leverage that content, offer it to well-trafficked media outlets. Syndicate your content using RSS feeds to spread your message and let news aggregators know when you have new content. (Don't forgo, however, an email alternative to an RSS subscription. The more ways you can spread and distribute your content, the better.)

You'll probably want to add the capability for visitors to tag content on your site with quick buttons and widgets. Your own blogs or website will link to positive mentions by others.

Being Experimental

I'm often asked by other entrepreneurs and business leaders about what the scale of their first social media engagement should be. Do we go in big to catch up? Should we design a small, careful trial? Is it reckless to take those first steps based on plain, old gut feel? But every business is different and I usually answer with the old Nike slogan: *Just do it!* There's much to gain and little to lose.

One of the distinct advantages of social media marketing is that it is very easy to experiment and adjust your tactics according to results that can be obtained very quickly. Whether you just want to get more traffic to your site or launch a complex, integrated campaign, you can afford to be experimental. If your message or offer shows good results, then by all means, expand the initiative. But when you don't see much reaction, either good or bad, a little patience may be in order. This is especially true for companies promoting niche products or complex service offerings. When it's difficult to find the influencers that can make a difference or when you have a complicated sales pitch, you must be willing to keep trying new combinations of messages and placement to gain new momentum.

This was a major theme at our last Lift conference. All the experts encouraged us to use trial and error to conduct experiments with various tools and media. Once you launch, expect to make tweaks and changes early and often. Once you identify what's working—do more of it!

Using All Channels

Any comment posted on Twitter, a blog, or a forum can make its way to the *Wall Street Journal*, and vice versa. It's vital to listen to all channels because you never know where a golden bit of information will appear. It's equally important to actively use all channels when communicating outbound to your customer base or a broader audience. You never know on what channel a potential customer or client will find out about you.

Though connected, each channel has its own protocol, its own purpose, etiquette, and temporal structure. Knowing how to use these channels is as important as knowing how to use each tool in a toolbox. You don't want to use a screwdriver where a wrench is needed, and you don't want to push a message across a channel devoted to UGC. Mapping these channels and understanding their role in the global communication structure is critical to making any plan work.

Trying Video

I've already admitted to being a huge advocate for video, so I'm not going to waste an opportunity for getting back up on my video soapbox. I'm frequently amazed at how effective video has become and how well it's faring in comparison to traditional advertising methods. I'm not the only one.

Proctor and Gamble, which certainly knows something about advertising, recently discovered the power of this new channel for a seventy-year-old brand. The P&G "The Man Your Man Could Smell Like" television commercial, featuring Isaiah Mustafa, went viral on the Internet, getting more than 30 million views on YouTube and boosting Old Spice sales by double digits.

P&G realized they had something, so they

executed a masterful social media marketing campaign. Over the course of two and a half days, the marketing minds behind the Old Spice brand posted 186 new videos to YouTube, featuring Mustafa answering questions from fans. The videos ranged from ten seconds long to just over a minute, with most of them in the thirty-second range. While that by itself is impressive, what's really amazing is that despite the size of P&G, their team produced these videos in real time, responding directly to comments made on various social media sites like Twitter, Facebook, and YouTube.

While most of us can only dream about getting the kind of reaction and cross-channel propagation that P&G received, there's a powerful incentive here for social media marketers to consider video. Don't be discouraged because you don't have actors on your payroll or the money or infrastructure to churn out Hollywood-perfect videos. With tools like smartphones, the ability to record a video is at everyone's fingertips and embedding and sharing video is second nature to many people these days. YouTube productions don't need to be super-slick or take a lot of resources. They just need to be engaging, and the messages should be short, clear, and relevant. I encourage you to formulate a plan to incorporate video into your marketing campaigns and customer relations activities. Who knows? Maybe you can create a level of Old-Spice-guy fandom by brainstorming creative engagement strategies. You won't know if you don't try.

The Education/Absorption Stage

By now you've introduced yourself, invited potential customers to your social profile sites and blogs, exchanged messaging, and begun to observe reactions and responses. You may have launched a few trial campaigns or be addressing many fronts in an effort to catch up. But this is the stage where you begin to understand the ins and outs of each of the major social platforms and start to appreciate the distinctions among community mind-sets. You've gotten a feel for what type of messaging is acceptable on certain sites and inappropriate on others, and you are learning to customize your message for the respective sites. You're also learning which multimedia messaging techniques your customers respond to best.

If customer service is important to your plan, you've tried social media as a means of complaint resolution or of proactive customer service and are likely seeing the potential for cost savings there. If yours is a business that might benefit from hyperlocal advertising, you've tested these waters also. You may have joined Yelp or Foursquare communities or tried a deal on

Groupon or another site. You're also now much more aware of what your competitors are doing with social media.

One of the most valuable parts of any company's social media self-education process, however, is discovering who the influencers are.

Identifying the Influencers

For decades, millions of Americans listened to Walter Cronkite as the trusted voice of the airwaves. This influential newscaster, and a handful of others, rose to fame at a time when the world had a finite number of communication channels and authority was the privilege of an elite set. Those days are gone. Today, there are millions of channels and an uncountable number of expert voices influencing any number of behaviors. Today influence can be subtle, like the rankings or ratings that influence the purchase of a coffee pot. Or influence can come by way of a concert of voices creating seismic shifts, like those that helped topple governments in Egypt and Tunisia. Knowing who wields influence around your brand today is as important as gaining an endorsement from Walter Cronkite might have been in yesteryear.

In today's interconnected world, one strong opinion can set off a cascade of sentiment in your favor or against you. That influencer takes many forms. Sometimes it's a well-respected content maven like Arianna Huffington. It may be one who rose from the rank and file, like Yelp's Miriam Warren, who, as a user, posted so many user reviews that she became a vice president of the company. Or, the influencer can simply be one who has ventured down a certain path before others. Unlike Cronkite, who broadcast his voice at fixed intervals, influencers today can shift and move with time or topic, by channel or demographic, wielding influence born from their experience, passion, or any number of characteristics that make their voices rise above the din.

In the online world, the key influencers may already be in your customer base. But they may not be. Influencers can be quite removed from the purchasing process, and may even be detractors who actively denigrate your industry. Influencers can be celebrities, bloggers, journalists, consultants, academics, or industry experts. Even lobbyists, regulators, and standards bodies can act as business influencers.

These influencers can be identified quantitatively—by the most tweets, likes, mentions, number of comments, etc. Traditional market research techniques and analysis tools can be helpful in identifying quantitative influence. Klout, the free Twitter influence-ranking tool, is especially useful. But influence is also contextual. Expertise needs to be relevant to a specific area or subject matter to effect views, decisions, or actions. We trust Warren Buffett's financial advice, but not necessarily his preference for pizza. And a quieter but trusted voice in a smaller, more concentrated network may actually drive more purchase behavior than that of a louder, more popular, celebrity.

Because the quality of the influence also matters, I think the best approach for identifying influence will always be a combination of analytics and the human brain. You'll also have to use your own eyes and knowledge to parse the conversation and identify influence in context.

Once you've begun to identify who your influencers are, you'll want to begin engaging with them in a way that recognizes their insight and expertise. Asking for their opinions or advice, linking to their own content assets, and offering them the first opportunity to try new products are just a few approaches.

Monitoring and Measuring

Listening is the first step in creating useful metrics that help align strategies and can dictate actions to communicate back to the consumer. Don't be overwhelmed by the amount of conversation or its diversity. Start by aligning listening practices with your strategic goals and categorize what you hear along those lines. You can then begin to identify key metrics for measurement that will be relevant to your business. The process involves listening to how company-generated messages resonate as well as marking the organic conversation that starts in social media. It also involves tracking that online activity back to the other established metrics that we'll discuss in Chapter 9. Listening without a goal is not very useful. Quantifying the aspects of conversations that are meaningful to your business gives you the ability to drive success from what you hear.

Collaborating

There can be a lot of excitement generated in the early stages of an organization's social media adoption. Unfortunately, a lot of internal competition can also arise. In big companies especially, the marketing, sales, IT, and customer service departments don't always work in concert anyway. And in companies new to the game, marketing tends to get the lion's share of resources and attention, crowding out or overshadowing the ideas or initiatives of other departments. That may be fine in the beginning, particularly if you're still experimenting with one-off campaigns. But you'll miss the full potential of that interconnected ecosystem if you don't start collaborating as a team.

Learning to collaborate is one of the biggest challenges of the early stages. The role of the CEO or other strategy leader is absolutely critical here in enabling cross-divisional cooperation, making sure that key players or departments don't get left out, and communicating that goals are company-wide, affecting and involving everyone.

The Growth Stage

Few companies will reach a true growth stage without full management buy-in because getting the most out of social media is a reflection of many commitments. One of them is definitely a commitment to ongoing engagement, which means quality content, and a plan for the allocation of time and resources for delivering it consistently and reliably. You may have a community manager, or a whole team of them, a few content creators, or a full-blown editorial department. The growth stage also assumes a commitment to ongoing reputation management and in this stage will include a very specific methodology for triaging complaints and platform-specific responses to particular situations. In the growth stage, for example, your own organization may decide to leverage that congenial Twitter expert who responds to mentions of your product and reaches out to offer technical assistance.

Finding Focus

In the growth stage you have begun to introduce relevance and focus into your strategy. The shotgun approach, while it brought with it a lot of learning, has yielded to specific approaches or branding campaigns for each social media tool you use and a methodology for linking them all together for the greatest visibility. You know where the influential dialogue takes place and are building relationships with influencers as a more focused use of time and resources. You've discovered your meaningful networks (and may have launched your own) and have established thought leadership positions. You're becoming proactive rather than merely reactive, using social media to generate leads and new business.

By now, you've done a lot of listening as well as tracking of your own online engagement. You may have established an outsourcing relationship, but there's data over a period of time to establish metrics. They're showing you where to concentrate activity and informing plans for scalability and expansion.

Defining Policy

If you haven't already crossed this bridge, the growth stage may require written policies for usage, level of transparency, content parameters, and employee participation. The policies that companies use to define employee participation can run the gamut from highly restrictive, spelling out rules that cover every type of online interaction, to very laissez-faire, where almost nothing is out of bounds.

I tend to favor the approach taken by Dell's CEO, Michael Dell. All Dell employees are allowed to comment on blogs that mention the company, so long as they use their own name and identify themselves as Dell employees. Since 2006, when Dell launched its DirectDell blog and online community initiative, online mentions of the company have gone from 50% to 20% negative.[37]

Obviously, the employees of a local bakery will have different legal vulnerabilities from the employees of an international bank. But some guidance should come from management or HR regarding the expectations on your staff for avoiding conflicts of interest and misrepresentation. See Chapter 10 for an in-depth discussion about some of the legal issues that these policies address.

Mainstreaming

Many companies will have made internal organizational changes that reflect and enable the commitments of the growth stage. At the very least, they will have allocated resources and determined who makes key decisions and who owns certain aspects of their social media strategy. For a real cultural change to take place, however, social media shouldn't be compartmentalized, or "over there" in its own little box in marketing, R&D, or customer service. I'm convinced that the full benefits of social media are realized only when it is mainstreamed into a company's own communications system, including those outward communications with its customer base. The efficiencies come when social media strategy comes out of its silo and into alignment with the business strategy. Social media becomes a game-changer when it becomes integrated with other marketing and communication channels across multiple departments to complement the company's overall mission.

By the growth stage your original plan will have been adapted and refined. Budget allocations can become realistic.

Conclusion

By way of summary, I'll describe the mature phase of an effective social media strategy. Its arrival may have come about after many months, or even years, of sustained engagement. There have been some false starts and mistakes. Some expectations didn't materialize, but others have astonished you. (That's one of the real thrills of social media—the amazing and far-reaching ripple effects that a small effort often returns.) But in a mature strategy model, you're not second-guessing anymore. You've stopped asking, "How long will it take before we see a return on our social media efforts?"

The Mature Stage

In this stage everyone in the organization is on board and vested in the continuing success of your social media initiatives. You've recruited writers, bloggers, and thought leaders from within the organization, and they represent a vital component of your online intelligence efforts. They are your in-house crowd sourcing resource, following your competitor's online efforts and offering suggestions for improving your own. It is often the case, however, with those companies that have listened well and created an actively engaged community, that the mature stage actually represents a decline in the demand for resources. As your social media strategy begins to take on a life of its own, fewer resources provide greater value and the focus shifts to supporting the community where your customers build and grow together.

In the mature stage, your social media approach to honesty and authenticity has pervaded your corporate culture, and your employees are proud to be part of a company that is active in using social media as a growth tool. You're also reaching out with education to other potential ambassadors within the virtual and physical communities through seminars, video, webinars, and podcasts.

You may be outsourcing your listening endeavors now, working with or without an agency, but your commitment to monitoring and measuring has definitely paid off. You have the data to know what you're getting from your social media campaigns and where you stand relative to your competitors.

Your social media identity is established and secure enough to be incorporated into traditional and offline marketing efforts. Customers are encouraged to "visit us on Facebook" in print media, business cards, and email signatures. Your marketing communications now flow seamlessly between the physical and digital worlds and a holistic, integrated strategy ensures that you are getting the cross-pollination that social media makes possible.

While your social media strategy may mature, it won't ever get old or stale. The platforms, tools, and channels will continue to go through technical change and popular turmoil, but in this stage you find that flux more exciting than intimidating. You know now that your strategies for participation will be constantly evolving. As your customers provide you with ongoing feedback, telling you, in their criticism and praise, how they use your brand or service and what features offer real value or need improvement, you're getting insight into the future of your business, from the biggest focus group the world has ever seen. The customer is no longer simply the "target" of your activity, but co-creative in developing strategies for the future.

To date there are not many companies whose social media usage has evolved to a fully effective, mature state. In a recent Harvard Review Business Analytic Services survey of 2,100 companies currently using social media, only a very small group—12 percent—of the companies surveyed said they felt they were currently effective users of social media. These were the companies most likely

- to have a strategy for social media use
- to deploy multiple channels
- to use metrics
- to integrate their social media into their overall marketing operations.[38]

I'm not at all surprised by the survey's findings. Those companies who arrive at a fully actualized, mature stage of social media use have embraced exactly these fundamentals.

While it may take some time, experimentation, and patience to get there, your mature strategy model will erase those doubts about social media's ability to increase visibility and profits. You'll be in the game to stay.

Chapter 8. A Group of Your Own: Building an Online Community

Member associations and user groups have been around a long time. Much longer than the World Wide Web. They were organized to do exactly what online communities, discussion forums, and user groups do today. Their members offered each other advice, asked and answered questions, and generally collaborated to share knowledge, concerns, and experiences. There was a huge social component of those communities, too. Members participated in swap meets, celebrated one another's personal and professional achievements, even created group buying opportunities. Many became vital, long-lasting associations. A user group begun in 1955 for IBM mainframe users in the aerospace industry is still active today.[39]

Most of those first user groups sprang up spontaneously around a good brand or product. (In the eighties, especially, there was a tremendous need for technical assistance with that new-fangled personal computer machine.) Many of these communities literally sustained themselves for decades without any official connection to the company that produced the product or service around which they were organized. And the companies who benefitted most from their existence seemed a little slow to realize that they were really missing a bet. One good example is Hewlett-Packard, a manufacturer of one of those new-fangled PC gadgets. HP didn't launch its customer support forum until February 2009. Within eighteen months of launch, however, the forum had recorded more than 100 million posts and registered 150,000 users. The forum also won a 2010 Star Award from the Technology Services Industry Association (TSIA) for Best Online Community.

With the new social Web, however, many companies are realizing that there's a lot of upside in taking the initiative themselves, rather than hoping that a group of users will do it on their own. They're creating company-sponsored, branded social communities to assist customers with product, service, and payment issues. They're providing environments where members, who are customers or likely prospects, make social contacts through collaboration and sharing.

Branded Communities

Building a branded community can be a risky proposition. One potential drawback of company-sponsored community initiatives is that visitors may perceive the community site as only another sales site for the company's marketing efforts. Visitors may make use of the information provided and exchanged, but they'll hold back in expressing their true feelings and opinions, and the community will fail to grow. Branded communities will lose credibility and traffic if they resemble true e-commerce sites. People don't join communities because they're looking for something to buy. They are looking for extensions of what is meaningful to them.

Many successful branded communities do provide significant value for both their members and the company. But they're not glorified e-commerce sites masquerading as member networks. They're places where users share commonalities well beyond the brand.

The goal of creating an online community is not unrelated to marketing goals. And a private, branded community allows for much more marketing flexibility than public social networks. But the community must have its own authentic reason for being. Nike's online community, for example, has a running and fitness lifestyle focus. Intuit community users come together to get help and to offer help with financial and tax issues. At Oraclecommunity.net, a site for people who are interested in Oracle's database and software products, members share personal stories, pictures, videos, and birthdays, and can even post their own blogs on the site.

There's no doubt that these communities drive product sales. But their members come together for much more than tennis shoes or software. When users don't perceive a true value proposition—for them, not the company—they'll stay away in droves.

Peer Member Communities

True peer member communities have sponsorship and sometimes commerce, but they are not specifically associated with a single corporate entity. These communities are built solely for the use and benefit of their members. They feature helpful content and offer great forums for member collaboration.

We have built two online communities in the past few years. I've already shared some of the experience of creating the ILD customer service forum—an experience which led directly to my own social media evangelism and the goal of writing this book. Our second site,

OfficeArrow, is a peer member community that originated out of our own fruitless search for a place dedicated to the specific needs of small office and business professionals.

With OfficeArrow we wanted to address the day-to-day issues that pull small business owners away from what is core to their business—the nearly universal problem of the baker who can't bake bread because he's overwhelmed with payroll, HR, finance, and accounting issues. Our tag line is "Where Busy People Come to Get Things Done," and we try to offer our members information, tools, and tips that enable them to manage these tasks faster and more efficiently. We offer articles on business management, finance, and human resources issues, career and office etiquette advice, document templates, a vocabulary building series, a virtual book club, and more.

We launched OfficeArrow three years ago, building it on a flexible technology platform that could grow and expand with the community. We started with a modest amount of relevant and authentic content that provided solutions to everyday problems, written in a style to which community members would relate. We recruited a core group of like-minded community members who became active very early on, starting discussions, asking and answering questions, and forming groups.

We also set out early on with a mission of monetizing social networking, which remains our focus to this day. Our OfficeArrow experience has shown that members expect to see advertising on the site as a way to underwrite the cost of the site and its content. We've found, however, that members are much more responsive to sponsor messages when they take the form of member newsletters or of funding the costs of webinars that feature expert content. Banner ads are certainly noticed by members, but the sponsorship of content and worthwhile product or service information is much more effective in engaging individual community members. We also offer group buying opportunities, delivered unobtrusively, for products and services chosen for their relevance to our members' interests.

This has been a bit of a learning curve for corporations and their respective agencies, but they are quickly gaining an understanding of the difference in advertising in an active member community environment versus traditional media. Knowing how to motivate interaction within social sites and member communities is a more comprehensive effort than merely buying banner ads. A network's value comes from its authenticity and from trust. Advertisers must not only be transparent, but they need to add value to the community.

The benefits come from gaining the trust of that much sought-after influencer group that active community members represent.

Building an online community from the ground up isn't easy. Like many social media endeavors, it requires patience and persistence and won't happen overnight, but there are many obvious rewards. A successful forum on your own domain will drive traffic to the site, create user-generated content for better search rankings, afford a wealth of ideas for product or service improvement, and create passionate, well-informed advocates for your brand. A peer member community can be customized to attract a valuable subset of social networkers who are not only eager to share views and information but are also open to marketing that caters to their specific needs and interests.

Member communities can come in many forms. Consumer social networks, peer member communities, and branded customer communities are closely related yet very different animals. Depending upon the type of community you're building, and the purpose behind it, the required learning will vary as you seek to understand what inspires dynamic conversations and shared experiences. Here are some tips we can pass on, based on our own research and a lot of trial and error, which will apply to all online communities.

Tips for Building an Effective Community

Have a Clear Focus

Communities, whether online or off, exist for a purpose. That purpose may be educational, political, religious, business, or something else. But being clear and focused in your reason for creating the community will enable you to carry that message throughout every element you build. Your focus should be broad enough to allow for a large field of discussion topics and for growth potential, yet narrow enough to carve out its own niche from public networks like Facebook. A focus of "gardening" may do that. A focus of "urban gardening" may do it better.

Even a quick tour of the successful niche social networks on the Internet will illustrate the importance of a focus that cuts participants out of the Facebook herd for an alternative or additional social networking experience. Care2 is a peer member community of users who are serious about green living. Gather, Eons.com, and BoomJ are sites that target older users, more likely to listen to NPR than the Top 40. Sosauce is a social networking platform for photo and travel enthusiasts. CarGurus attracts automotive hobbyists. The list goes on and on.

Even branded communities, as we've seen, fare better when the focus is not overtly on the brand or service, but a related passion, interest, or need that also binds the members.

Determine to Offer Real Value

The focus of your community will enable you to offer something of clear value. I'm not talking about the value to you as the owner that necessarily generates revenue. I'm talking about the value that your community offers to its members. You may have to dig deep to understand the underlying needs and motives of your specific user group. Listening actively to online conversations of your potential users will reveal where they're openly asking for advice, what they're angry or excited about, or where they're just frustrated. The goal of providing genuine value to the users, not the company or advertisers, should guide all decisions, from usability to content. Revenue generation and ROI discussions are entirely valid, but they're putting the cart before the horse. If user needs are put first, I believe the value will emerge.

Design It for the Users

Users care much less about the aesthetics of a site than they do its utility. If you study the most successful sites on the Web, you'll see that they're simple but user-friendly. Fancy buttons, peculiar images, and unconventional navigation are not as likely to impress users as they are to drive them away. It's important for visitors to spot the latest activity, and the technique for posting should be especially obvious and easy. Ensure that new post buttons are prominent and clearly labeled. You don't want contributors to leave your site because they didn't know how to post.

There is no formulaic solution here. Early on, you need to spend time understanding your user. Craft a "persona" of the ideal member and then prepare one or more use cases to capture how users will navigate your site. If possible, test the design with some focus groups to get their reactions. Time and money spent at this stage will save you in the long run.

Assign and Empower a Forum Administrator or Community Manager

Perhaps the single most important element for a thriving online community is an alert, dedicated manager. The manager of a branded community needs to be able not only to answer questions but also to facilitate conversation among other community members. He or she needs to operate like a great host or hostess, making newbies comfortable, introducing members to one another, and seeing that members' needs are met, whether that's in the form of an answer to their question or in connecting them to an activity they can participate in. The community administrator will also be responsible for monitoring those posts that come from far left field. Nothing scares away users like a bunch of random posts that make the site look unfocused and cluttered.

Sure, you can hire an agency to manage your community, but I don't think an agency can take the place of a dedicated employee. And if you're running a customer support forum, that employee better know your product or service inside and out.

Offer a Variety of Content and Keep It Fresh

Even customer service forums don't have to be dry and boring. FAQs, how-to articles and videos, and customer satisfaction polls can support the knowledge base and make the site more interesting and informative. On member sites, webinars are hugely popular and promote engagement. Guest writers can contribute thought leadership. Surveys, and their results, are interesting to participants and advertisers alike.

Set a publishing schedule and stick to it. Keep the content coming and keep it fresh. Nothing is as off-putting as going to the site to find the last post is dated weeks or months ago. And stale content will not keep you on the first page of a Google search. You'd be surprised how quickly your search results will suffer if you don't keep fresh posts coming.

We're still building our OfficeArrow community, but some of our most successful content included informational webinars, how-to videos, and real-life stories from experts that connected with the audience and spurred conversations and discussions.

Start Slowly and Build It Authentically

You can create a great site, endow it with tons of features, set up threads for dozens and dozens of great topics, and then absolutely nothing happens. It's a little like arriving too early for a party. You're reluctant to go in. You wait around, sit in the car, hoping someone else will show up to ring the doorbell first. It's a problem, and one made worse by overzealous preparation. There are certainly things you can do to prepare for the launch of a new community and to invite folks to the party. Media announcements, press releases and email campaigns are just some of the ways to send out invitations. But an overly complicated design, a hundred empty threads, and heavy marketing hype can make a new site look like the unstarted party or the empty restaurant. At the very beginning, you may even want to forgo vendor content or marketing.

In preparing this chapter, I discovered a terrific website called *The Online Community Guide*, run by Richard Millington, who is an online community consultant. The site offers a wealth of good tips and is a great resource if you're thinking about building a community.

In one post entitled, "The Amateur Approach to Building Online Communities," Richard offers some advice that's just too good not to quote in its entirety:

> Amateurs have natural advantages. The founder(s) usually begin with a good number of contacts in the sector, they're fully committed to the project, they know what sort of discussions to start, what content to write, and have a good number of existing friends who share their interest. They know the community they're trying to start will work—because it's the sort of community they want to participate in.
>
> Most importantly, they don't have any ulterior motive other than to create a fun community for members. Members never feel manipulated.
>
> Brands need to adopt the amateur approach. Forget the explosive growth and persuasive messages. Start small. Have real employees making real friends among your audience before you begin—at least 50. Start discussions you know your audience will be interested in (often

discussions about them) and ask them to participate.[40]

I think this is sound advice, both in its emphasis on taking your time and on authenticity. You really can't "message" your way through it. Communities have an amazing ability to ferret out the fake. They are interactive and built on real discussions and personal exchanges. Don't fight it. That's the beauty of what you are building.

Recognize and Reward Users

We all love recognition and status and there are a variety of ways to acknowledge contribution in peer member communities. Badges, special designations, points, and rewards can be used to reward participation and can also work as a referral strategy for helping the community grow. *Huffington Post* has used this system very effectively. Their badges, running from "Networker" to "Predictor" recognize users in the three key areas of connecting with others, engaging with content, and moderating comments. (*Huffington Post* ties its own social community to the Facebook and Twitter communities. Mashable has copied the same model.)

In our own OfficeArrow community, we also recognize and designate members based on their participation levels (questions asked, answers given, discussion posts, etc.) as "Spectators," "Experts," and even as "Superheroes," but we also recognize personal member achievements and even birthdays.

Contests, quizzes, and special events can also recognize members while promoting a sense of community and fun. Don't hesitate to try them, even if your community is very serious in nature. On the second anniversary of OfficeArrow, we had a giveaway every thirty minutes, and the only requirement was that you come wish us a happy birthday. We had scores of members on the site all day, some offering lengthy birthday wishes and suggestions for continued success. Imagine that! A whole day of user feedback with a fun overlay.

Let the Debates Happen

The liveliest, most vital communities are those whose members feel free to express themselves, even on controversial subjects, or on points that don't necessarily reflect your brand in its most positive light. Good debates are vital for successful communities, and it's even fun sometimes to stir the pot a little. We generated an "iPhone vs. BlackBerry" debate on our site that extended for well over a year and generated some very intense opinions.

You can certainly have some rules and guidelines. (These should be clearly posted and unambiguous.) And you need a moderator who's paying attention. Moderators are well within their rights in removing posts with language that is too colorful or abuses other members. The previous chapter's guidelines for playing nice in social media apply here, too. Moderation and control are necessary to keep the discussions in line and not let your community get hijacked, but you have to do it with restraint. The give-and-take of open debate generates interest and creates passionate users.

Encourage Segmentation

Allowing the formation of groups and subgroups within the user community will benefit users, sponsors, and content creators. These smaller peer groups can generate intense social bonding and target overlooked issues of importance to the community. They open opportunities for collaborative learning and teaching and create, by extension, great user-generated content. Members who start groups or act as group moderators often have strong network ties and a high degree of community respect, thus also self-identifying as important influencers. Look no further than LinkedIn for proof that segmentation works.

I generally prefer allowing users to form their own groups rather than having a site administrator create arbitrary categories or buckets of association. But if your users don't do it themselves, you might consider setting up some form of geographic segmentation. Geographic segmentation opens up possibilities for members to meet facc-to-face, extending the sharing and socializing into the offlinc world.

Conclusion

While some of the largest and most enduring online user communities were created by passionate users themselves, many companies arc now realizing that theie's a lot to gain by aligning themselves with communities whose members represent customers or prospective customers.

We all share the need to collaborate with those like us on some basis, and with the size and scope of the Internet, online communities represent the virtual extension of real-time telephonic or face-to-face discussions and meetings organized around people who share the same beliefs, desires, or goals. The ability to engage and be involved in communities and forums that provide user-generated comment and firsthand experiences from a network of trusted peers is powerful.

The recent rapid growth in online communities, fueled by the technology that facilitates them, is truly an amazing development, likely to continue as smartphones and tablet devices continue to proliferate.

Your customers may already be tipping you off that you're ready for a brand-centric community. You may choose, as we did, to fill a known void with a peer member community.

I don't think, however, that even branded communities have to be limited to enterprise corporations with enormous marketing budgets. When you combine the low cost of readily available applications with mobile technology, there's really no reason that even the local coffee shop can't have its own vibrant community and enthusiastic membership.

The process may be a little slow out of the gate. It can take some time to build a user base and to discover the mix of information and fun that makes the user experience most worthwhile. But a little patience, a clear focus on purpose, and a commitment to delivering authentic value for your members are the fundamentals for success.

Chapter 9. Meaningful Metrics

Social media holds the promise of many new opportunities for promoting our businesses, acquiring new product ideas, and improving customer service. But it also changes fast, has a lot of moving parts, and there are many ways to be analyzed and measured. The path to the "bottom line" doesn't seem as straightforward and direct in social media as it did in more established sales and marketing practices. Nervous executives look at some of the obvious indicators of social media success and wonder what these phenomena really mean. Suppose we do generate a lot of Twitter traffic. What if we do acquire thousands of Facebook fans? Does that mean anything at all relative to the real bottom line? What does it mean even to the ROI of my relatively small social media budget?

I am an old school, value-oriented, ROI-focused executive myself. I understand, particularly in today's economy, that we all have to pay close attention to how we invest our shareholders' money. I don't like to guess about the impact of investment in new strategies or initiatives. And even with traditional media I've been suspicious myself of the real effects of marketing campaigns. Like many of you I have laughed uncomfortably at the old saying, "Half of our advertising works; we just don't know which half."

I do appreciate the skepticism. The reality is that there are few absolutes in measuring any business initiative. But I'm convinced that where social media is held up against traditional media, that skepticism is largely misplaced. Through the use and application of social media marketing tools, today's marketing and finance disciples have access to more data than at any point in history. These tools not only produce near real-time data, but they can help us process and analyze it for highly actionable ROI metrics. It's now possible to measure social media with far greater accuracy than efforts in traditional media.

Tying Metrics to Revenue

With every emerging technology, a new array of metrics appears. Social media is no different. Most of the professional analytics experts practicing in the social media space want you to believe that the new metrics they introduce are the ones that will catapult your business to the next level. In reality, most of these metrics are fabricated to validate their services and have little bearing on success. These "new" metrics create a lot of noise and often obscure real measurements of success. There is no doubt that the most meaningful metric will always be revenue. But it is possible to find other grounded metrics, tied to revenue, that business leaders can use to create predictive models for optimal use of social media.

To measure most effectively, leaders need to align active listening with strategic goals and then calibrate those goals with paid media (the media you buy), earned media efforts (the attention generated by others), and site traffic. All media activities can then be mapped to near-term, midterm, and long-term goals.

In the classroom at The Wharton School, University of Pennsylvania, Steve Ennen's Marketing Advanced Study Project class was tasked with finding meaningful measurements for online conversations that can relate to various business objectives, across any

industry. Using Social Strategy1 and the examples of
global brands, they worked with communications and
branding firms Porter Novelli and BBDO. The resulting
research identified metrics, rooted in traditional business,
that will prove enduring and can lead directly to return
on investment for near-term goals, like sales or
influence, and longer-term goals, like reputation
management.

Reach

One key metric verified by the Wharton research
is *reach*—how far content (e.g., a topic, subject, or
meme) spreads across the totality of the Internet. Reach
emphasizes the importance of tracking conversations
about your brand across everything from Forbes.com to
Foursquare, because each channel is connected to—and
can influence users on—every other channel. That
mapping is critical in determining how these
conversations influence dynamics like brand affinity or
the likelihood of purchase.

Reach is important to both paid and earned media
efforts. In the paid media ranks, reach gives us a sense of
whether our campaigns are resonating with our target
audience or falling flat. Because messages, memes, and
other conversations can spread much farther across the
Internet than in analog media, reach becomes a very

important measurement. One concrete example of this came by way of a tweet discovered by Social Strategy1 in which a young person claimed to have been fired illegally from a global firm. That singular tweet was picked up by a blog, spread to a job forum, and eventually moved all the way to a professional online community of tens of thousands. Like a snowball rolling downhill, this little tweet acquired significant mass in terms of impressions or online "eyeballs." Only by measuring the reach of a conversation can we know the real impact it may be having on our brand or company.

An increase in reach may chart to a growing impact on brand awareness, advocacy, loyalty, purchases, and many other established consumer behaviors. In fact, the extent to which noteworthy content is being relayed or passed on by consumers may give us more insight than a traditional measurement like response to a TV advertisement. We know that while only 14% of consumers trust advertising, some 78% of them trust peer recommendations. This means that, by a factor of 6:1, reach may be a more important, more valid metric than some of the widely accepted Web measurements.

By tying total Internet reach to established metrics, we have solid footing on which to measure the impact of the content shared around your brand. We are all probably aware that unique visitors and page views (the number of times a Web page is served) are important measurements of our Web traffic. When measuring online activity in general, we want to look at whether the increase (or decrease) in reach has a direct impact on your site. It should. In working with Social Strategy1 clients, it has become clear that the best measurement strategy should allow you to map connections between online conversation, other aspects of your messaging efforts (earned or paid), and conversion activity on your sites against brick-and-mortar operations.

Often, reach is instrumental in "discovery" or the ability for customers, new or old, to find you at their point of need. Marketers have long known that search is the second step in the purchase process (recognition of need is the first), so the ability to be discovered through strong reach can have a direct impact on sales. Additionally, by drawing connections between these measures, we can correlate reach to on-site or in-store conversion activity. As far as I am concerned, reach is a critical factor in knowing how much impact that content or conversation, good or bad, can have on your business.

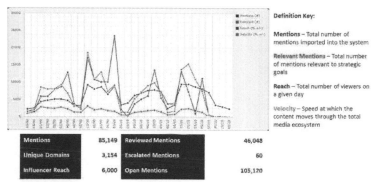

Mentions	85,149	Reviewed Mentions	46,048
Unique Domains	3,154	Escalated Mentions	60
Influencer Reach	6,000	Open Mentions	105,120

Definition Key:

Mentions – Total number of mentions imported into the system

Relevant Mentions – Total number of mentions relevant to strategic goals

Reach – Total number of viewers on a given day

Velocity – Speed at which the content moves through the total media ecosystem

Figure 1. *The histogram above illustrates the change in volume (reach) of an online conversation around a brand, based on percentage change, day over day. By watching changes in reach, one can pinpoint the theme of the messages affecting readers. Velocity represents the speed at which the content moves across the Internet. By measuring these elements together, one can establish a baseline for ROI by understanding whether the messages are resonating.* **Courtesy of Social Strategy1**

Velocity

Another important measurement is *velocity*, or the speed at which a conversation moves across the Internet. Steve Ennen's classroom work at Wharton also identified the velocity metric as vital to determining whether a hot-button issue is brewing (like a great deal, a product recall, or a pricing or service issue), whether marketing efforts are working, how quickly a product, service, or marketing message is adopted or shared; and, as importantly, crisis communications or management. Velocity can also measure the relationship between earned and paid media efforts and if any uptick in activity aligns with company-generated messages.

Measuring velocity in concert with reach offers a very basic connection to ROI: Are my efforts resonating with the consumer? Is the seven-figure ad creating awareness? Are people misconstruing my message? Are they talking about the competition's campaigns, meaning my money is wasted? We can now hear firsthand the answers to these questions.

The Voice of the Customer

As we examine the phenomenon of social networks, it's easy for us to look at the global scale and scope of the traffic and miss the fact that the postings, reviews, and commentary from our customers are incredibly powerful metrics in themselves. The best indication of how well our marketing or other business efforts are faring comes directly from the voice of the customer. And we now have the power to hear every comment posted by these customers. When customers share their feelings on the same topic, or with the same sentiment about our brands, we can measure that sentiment and the reach or velocity of that conversation.

When CFOs speak to marketers, there is often a disconnect between the branding efforts and ROI perspectives. By quantifying customer viewpoints such as tone, sentiment, advocacy, or disapproval, and measuring reach, velocity, discovery, and conversion behavior in the total media environment, CMOs can track which of their efforts is resonating with the buying public. There is nothing more powerful than a verbatim comment from a customer. If one hundred comments track the same way, we have actionable insight.

From the marketing perspective, we can measure how customers respond to ad campaigns. Is the key message in your campaign resonating with consumers? Is the language right and the message clear? Does it drive others to purchase? Through careful analysis, we can determine if a target audience likes the product or campaign based on what they say and do online. This aligns with the traditional metrics of "frequency response functions," which model the reaction of a population to exposure of advertising.

So, how do we quantify each comment or the total conversation and tie that to a meaningful measurement? By aggregating, cataloging, and analyzing the linguistic markers of the conversations, as well as how those conversations move across the social and mainstream media channels, we can enable business leaders to quantify the influence of issues/content on customer behavior. This process allows us to be responsive, even predictive, in our outreach to the consumer or customer. This predictive ability comes from the smart use of tools never before available, yet it doesn't lead us too far away from established business practices. Historically, we couldn't know how people felt about our ads or the color of a toaster. In the past we tried to determine this feedback through focus groups that may have corralled 20 to-30 folks, or through our attempts to tie a possible correlation with sales—neither of which measure on the large scale. Now we can hear not only the voice of each customer, but how the total chorus feels about that color or ad, enabling us to make real-time adjustments.

Measuring the Super Bowl Buzz

As an experiment in tracking reach, velocity and sentiment, Social Strategy1 examined the effectiveness of Super Bowl advertisers, to analyze the staying power of commercials shown during the event, based on social media buzz. We first looked at the game day social media buzz of the commercials. We then tracked those same ads for the following week to determine which ones had made lasting impressions. Finally, we attempted to generate insight from the conversations themselves, looking at what people were actually saying about the ads and their sponsoring brands. We reviewed hundreds of thousands of actual mentions and conversations, looking not only for the buzz winners and losers, but also at whether the ad resonated with the intended audience. Did the audience respond in ways the advertisers likely wanted them to respond? In other words, did the audience get it? The results were extremely interesting and not always consistent with the results we saw from other media sources.

In looking at this data from the single ad group, it is clear that Chrysler scored big during the game with its "Imported from Detroit" commercial with Eminem. Not only did it cause meaningful buzz, but also in those conversations where sentiment was projected, it was more than 93% positive. This ad created an emotional connection unlike any other. There were thousands of conversations like this:

> "That Chrysler commercial actually gave me a chill."

> "Dude, I am all about that Chrysler ad. Kinda makes you believe that Detroit *will* rebuild. Nice."

In addition, there were conversations that appeared to inspire people to purchase, like these:

> "OMG! I loved the Chrysler 200 commercial with Eminem! I loooove the car too! I am 100% sure that will be my next car!!!"

> "Liked that Chrysler commercial ... Motor
> City... Makes me want a 200."

The Chrysler ad was a direct score. It resonated with the audience, provided a good feeling about the brand and city, and appeared to inspire people to want to purchase. Home run.

On the flip side, however, Groupon's first entry into Super Bowl TV advertising was a dud. While the Groupon commercial did cause a reasonable amount of buzz, the sentiment was largely negative. In fact, it was one of only two companies or brands whose sentiment was more than 50% negative, coming in at 56% negative. Most of the negative sentiments looked like these:

> "So is Groupon making fun of genuinely
> unfortunate situations? I don't get it."

> "Groupon ad: Screw Tibet, save money on fish
> curry."

Some even mocked the Groupon business model:

> "That @groupon commercial? 50% off having a
> clue how to spend millions on a Super Bowl
> spot."

While most found the ads offensive, audience

responses like the last entry do show that the brand and its business model is widely known.

Certain commercials, while not necessarily creating tons of buzz relative to other brands, did seem to resonate with their target audience. One of the brands that seemed to win in this regard was Audi. It was clear that their audience got the essence of the commercial as seen in conversations like this one:

> "Escape the confines of old luxury. Audi, well done."

The commercial will also likely lead to the action that the company was looking for as seen is conversations like these:

> "I want an Audi A8..."

> "The Audi A8 is so sexy."

Another interesting observation that arose from reviewing these conversations was that there was a higher level of sophistication with these mentions, less slang, fewer "lol's" and other social acronyms which would indicate that the ad was hitting an older demographic and likely its target audience.

By matching this overall customer sentiment and its reach to daily, weekly, or monthly marketing spend, we have for the first time a direct link between push communications and ROI. It is therefore possible to draw connections to what we call "brand affinity" and its direct impact on the value of brands. If we add customer service costs to this picture—costs which are often reduced by communicating directly through the social media channels, then you can start to see how active listening can map to revenue and cost structure. Quantifying the conversation gives us an overview of sentiment and customer intent or advocacy toward those brands and can help us understand how to nurture the value of the customer asset.

Here are questions that can be answered by listening to the voice of the customer:

- Are customers discussing concepts about your company that align with the concepts you want them to discuss?
- Are consumers advocating the products and services you offer to their friends and connections?
- If there is advocacy, how many connections are there; and what are the drivers behind the reach and velocity as this passes from user mode to user mode?

Using these questions as a basis for monitoring, we can quantify the conversations, creating a direct link to ROI for paid media or to drivers behind earned media. This helps companies become more predictive and prescriptive in their communications efforts. In addition to being a great predictive tool for buying behavior, this process is also an indicator of the perception of your brand and the effectiveness of your customer service.

Figure 2. The data in the graph below was captured by Social Strategy1 in its analysis of the 2011 Super Bowl ads. The x-axis of the graph shows the reach of the mentions/conversations, the relative size of the bubbles represents the buzz (the number of mentions), and the movement along the y-axis represents the relative positive versus negative sentiment of the mentions.

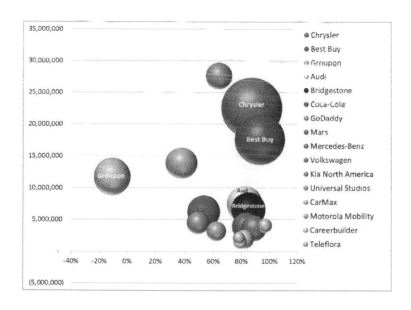

Customer Lifetime Value

All of these measures directly relate to Customer Lifetime Value (CLV) calculations. We know customer lifetime value helps us arrive at the dollar value of the long-term relationship with any given customer, revealing how much that customer will spend (or is worth) over a given period of time. By listening to customers en masse and breaking out buying components such as rankings, ratings, reviews, recommendations, loyalty, and advocacy, we have more data available to draw CLV insights and predict switching costs and churn. In my discussions with CEOs, CMOs, and e-commerce executives in general, the most essential number for them is the customer lifetime value expressed in dollars and cents. This is our collective holy grail.

Part and parcel of customer lifetime value is our weighted average cost of customer acquisition. By actively listening to and monitoring consumer behavior we can draw a tighter connection between paid and earned media and how much impact those efforts have on customer acquisition. The question becomes: Can we decrease customer acquisition cost by increasing our earned media reach and discovery? Absolutely. Businesses now have a great selection of measuring and monitoring tools to utilize in calculating customer acquisition costs.

Formerly, we had to rely on ad costs divided by number of customers acquired for our acquisition metrics. In social media, customers become active advocates or adversaries of our brands, influencing the decisions of other customers and figuratively raising their hands while doing so. Customers also discuss their purchases online and recommend or dissuade others from making the same purchases or contracting for services. These sentiments spread, measurably. By listening to these conversations, businesses can also identify key influencers talking about the brand and map that online chatter, activity, and reach to site traffic or sales, thereby refining CLV and customer acquisition calculations using the same dynamics. Customers who are more vocal or active around a brand and have a high number of others who respond to their messages are great indicators of user influence and can offer a more complete picture of how online and offline marketing or branding efforts are affecting the customer base.

By working a simple equation based on average spend-per-purchase and number of purchases per year, as well as the customer retention rate tied to these social media metrics, you can truly quantify the impact of online conversations and the way they favorably or unfavorably impact CLV, customer acquisition, customer retention, and brand loyalty.

Activity alone is an important measure of how your brand is viewed. Traditionally, we thought of brand affinity as likelihood to purchase, but in social media that takes other forms that have direct impact on sales. Loyalty and advocacy are huge factors when you identify just how your brands or products are viewed in the media ecosystem. They can also identify key nodes for brand-generated messaging, giving us the tools to cut paid media costs by leveraging these channels and nodes.

Mapping to Other Metrics

As I've outlined, the Internet has enabled a lot of key metrics that can generate deeper, more insightful data on our business. What business leaders need to do is tie those metrics together for the complete performance picture. Let's return to the basics.

Unique Visitors and Page Views

When we drive customers to our sites, we give them the label of *unique visitors*. How much they consume on these sites is measured by *unique page views*. Therefore, the number of unique viewings of our site is important to understanding how much traffic we are generating through earned or paid media efforts and how much interest is being generated by the content or information on the site. Once on the sites we want some sort of activity that can increase revenue, spark a conversion behavior, or seed engagement—the long-term or short-term relationship visitors have with the site and the brand. (It's important to note that time spent on a site is not always a measure of this engagement. Sometimes users just want to get in and out, buy and be gone.)

In the practice of paid media (the dollars we spend on getting people to our sites), we often drive traffic through purchased ads on a cost-per-click (CPC) basis. These are generally measured by ad costs divided by number of clicks generated. Once visitors are on the site or en route to the site, we are measuring an activity: the conversion.

Cost-per-Order

Cost-per-order, another conversion activity, can measure the cost-effectiveness of advertising by measuring ad costs divided by the number of orders generated. These are strong measurements that can be added to our calculations for cost-per-acquisition. By adding the earned media component—essentially what people are saying about your brand, how that increases reach and discovery (and therefore traffic)—and linking that to these other metrics, we can crack the elusive advertising and promotion ROI.

From various social media sites such as blogs,

social networks, forums, etc., the raw number of followers and supporters can provide reasonable benchmarks of your extended network, and tracking that to conversion activity creates insight into your brand awareness and affinity across the broader ecosystem. For example: A Facebook ad may spark a conversation among the fans of that page and spread to another consumer forum, then trickle back to your home site, on which 500 people convert. Mapping the drivers of this conversation then gives you ROI and CPA data points.

These can become very tactical measurements, but rolled into a strategic viewpoint and incorporating active listening as a measure of performance, you can see the possibilities integrating the newer media channels with the foundations of sales generation. We've been concentrating on the consumer, too. If we take a few steps back and start to examine the entire ecosystem, we see a lot more in terms of marketplace, market shifts, trends, and opportunities.

Beyond the Customer

There are other, more complex business issues, while not directly related to customer acquisition costs or CLV, that monitoring tools can also illuminate. From an investing standpoint, for example, monitoring can identify conversations around start-ups or established brands as they prepare for new phases of growth or sell-offs. You'd be surprised at the amount of conversation that bankers, buyers, and others create around the investment process. By using the same tools we outlined for brand management, investors can derive a detailed overview of investment criteria that add to the due diligence of traditional investing processes. Already, popular media is touting the use of Twitter by general investors, but there is far more to using social media in financial services than Twitter-tips. By quantifying these conversations we can actually measure how customers feel about the target company's product, service, price, management, etc., measure the activity, or volume of these conversations, and map those back to consumer behavior. Just as the examples above, if we see a groundswell of support or favor behind a fledgling company, an investor can determine that there is likely a bright future for that company in the midterm. It's not hard to see how the metrics we established in our work with Wharton can translate into investment tools.

Conclusion

In this chapter, I've tried, on a broad and general basis, to demonstrate how to establish concrete measurements that connect online user behavior to your business. My goal was to mitigate some of the concerns that business leaders might have about the inability to tie social media initiatives to the real bottom line and to the traditional metrics with which they're familiar. The new listening and monitoring technologies are eliminating much of the guesswork that have clouded marketing expenditures, now making it possible to gauge the success of social media initiatives even more accurately than those of traditional media. Beyond the customer, these same tools can also provide us with valuable intelligence to inform traditional investment and financial decisions.

As a word of caution, however, there are four general mistakes made in measurement, no matter what you measure. Those failures are:

- Companies fail to pull comments from the entire media spectrum.
- Information is ineffectively shared within the organization. It's important to ensure that all of these metrics are woven into the organization as a whole. Everyone in the strategic process needs to know.
- Goals and the metrics themselves are poorly defined. You should not be spending money or building campaigns just to bring people to your site. You should be bringing people to your site

with a specific goal in mind.

- Companies either don't take action or take improper action on results. Measuring results alone isn't enough. Success lies in communicating the metrics and goals back into your sales and marketing process.

It's definitely possible to know when your social media marketing is working. By clearly defining goals, deriving meaningful metrics that connect to those goals, and communicating the results throughout the organization, overall strategy and individual campaigns can be evaluated and fine-tuned in an ongoing process that goes straight to the bottom line.

Chapter 10. Compliance, Governance, and Reporting

As you already know, I'm a true sales and marketing guy, so I'd much rather focus on the marketing and growth aspects of social media—how it can help us prospect for and retain customers and analyze ways to expand by launching new products and services. These activities, however, are just much harder to address when you're bogged down by legal, accounting, or regulatory compliance issues. Social media has already begun to influence many other corporate functions beyond sales and marketing. It is already changing the ways that we manage our financial reporting, regulatory compliance, corporate governance, and human resources activities.

We all operate in a very litigious and, in my opinion, a highly overregulated business environment. But as business owners and executives, we can have no illusions about the importance of complying with all those laws and regulations. Nor can we ignore the demands and expectations of our boards of directors, our shareholders, customers, partners, and lenders to operate not just morally and ethically, but with an absolute commitment to accurate reporting.

Many business leaders are posing questions about how the social media revolution will change employee relations, compliance, governance, and financial reporting. Some of the questions they're asking include:

- What role will social media play in our responsibilities for proper financial reporting?
- How will it affect management's reporting to our board of directors and otherwise influence the practice of good corporate governance?
- What changes will social media bring about in the relationships between businesses and their legal counsels, accountants, and with other professionals such as consultants and contractors?
- What new legal issues or pitfalls has social media created for companies and individuals?

- What policies for employee usage of social media should we implement to protect our companies and our employees?

The answers to these questions—and the changes that some of them imply—will involve more than the marketing and sales teams. The expansion of social media has raised new issues and concerns across the organization. Management, accounting, legal, and human resources all have obligations to acknowledge these new issues and to create policies for addressing them.

The Legal Aspects of Social Media

To understand how some of the known issues are being addressed and to speculate about what new ones may be on the horizon, I reached out to Ed Brown of the law firm of Burr & Forman. Ed is vice chairman of the firm's business law section and has been very hands-on in managing social media issues for his firm and his clients. The following is a question-and-answer session I recently had with Ed.

Q: Ed, before we discuss the issues that relate to your providing help and insight to your clients, it would be great, especially for readers who represent professional entities, to get a little of your own background. When did you first become aware of social media? Was there a particular moment or event that was associated with this initial awareness?

A: Not long ago, I was asked by three separate clients to work on transactions that involved "mobile content delivery networks." At about the same time, it seemed that everyone started to discuss the "cloud." Suffice it to say that I was more than a bit confused. I had only a vague notion of what a "mobile content delivery network" might be, and absolutely no idea to what "cloud" they were referring. I realized that my children were much more in tune with these terms than I was. Within two weeks, I had joined LinkedIn and Facebook, and purchased a smartphone.

While I knew you didn't need a smartphone to use LinkedIn or Facebook, it seemed that smartphones were expanding the use of social media sites exponentially. While the staples of social media were launched in 2003 (LinkedIn), 2004 (Facebook), and 2006 (Twitter), it seemed that the introduction of the iPhone by Apple set the social media world on fire by giving immediate access to the social media network. With that came "mobile content delivery networks" and the "cloud." I doubt my life will ever be the same.

Q: Can you describe your firm's current and planned social media initiatives?

A: To be honest, law firms are not generally known as leaders in technology or early adopters. We are still tied to physical offices and an organizational structure that has basically remained unchanged since I began practicing law in 1980. It took law firms years to accept that the Internet was anything but a potential waste of time for employees. Now we're trying to determine how to use social media to our advantage, and that will take time. We won't be putting ads on Facebook or giving "two-for-ones" on Groupon. The decision makers to whom we target our efforts may be involved in social media, but so far they are not making their law firm decisions based solely on campaigns.

At Burr & Forman, we are trying to identify the best uses for social media. Instead of just placing a link on our website, social media permits us to distribute information directly to clients and potential clients in a more efficient manner than before. We also look at our clients' presence on social media sites, as well as that of our attorneys who are using social media.

Q: How do your clients use social media, and are they influenced by the types of social media that you use?

A: We look to our employees who are already savvy when it comes to using these networks to help push our message. Decision makers are being hired at younger ages and in turn are more adept at using social media to assist them in making various decisions, including which law firm to hire. We're also using the information gathered by Social Strategy1 as intelligence to learn more about our competitors.

While we may not be leading the way, we are committed to looking forward rather than backward. For example, we're training lawyers on how to use LinkedIn to connect with current and potential clients, and we're creating a Facebook page for the firm. We've had the most fun by launching a radio program, "Results Matter Radio."It allows us to give exposure to our lawyers while at the same time providing a platform for our clients, colleagues, and friends to be interviewed and to spread their message as well. We record the show for broadcast, but also make it available as a podcast that we can distribute not only through our website, but through LinkedIn, Twitter, and Facebook.

Q: What sort of inquiries are you getting from your clients about social media?

A: Not surprisingly, the questions that arise are widespread. Many are about creating policies to control or limit access to the Internet or social media at the workplace, and questions involving privacy issues and the right of the employer to view social media content. These are the types of questions that have been around since the advent of the Internet. With the advent of the smartphone, however, these questions will likely become less common. The use of the smartphone as the preferred device for connecting to social media has made it virtually impossible for an employer to control employee access.

With the advent of the smartphone, clients are becoming concerned with employees inadvertently distributing information about a prospective customer, product pricing, etc. In the past, we were only concerned about the employee who might have a few too many drinks at a party and talk a bit too much to a few friends who probably had just as much to drink. Now, however, when an employee tweets the same information or places it on Facebook, the entire world has access to the information. We regularly see news stories about employees being terminated for saying inappropriate things on Twitter or another site. There was a wonderful line in *The Social Network* that went, "the Internet isn't written in pencil, it's written in ink." Employers are beginning to focus on developing policies to help employees manage their use of social media.

Social media presents unique challenges for employers because of the types of information employees or potential employees may post on such sites and the ability of employers to view such information in a publicly accessible forum. For example, an employer may not discriminate against a union affiliate or sympathizer by not hiring the applicant based upon the individual's union support or status discovered on his or her social media page.

Q: How are you raising awareness with your clients in regard to social media?

A: Because we're lawyers, we often come bearing bad news, or warnings about what might happen. This is certainly true in the case of social media. For those clients that are not on the cutting edge, we have begun to reach out to them about establishing reasonable policies and practices within their company.

A company that ignores social media rather than determining how it fits in with the company's culture runs the risk of allowing its employees to adversely impact its business by making social media statements that disclose trade secrets, malign competitors and other employees—or worse, make statements that are derogatory about the company. Clients need to be aware of the types of messages its employees are sending via social media, and need to give serious thought to the types of messages they may want to restrict or encourage. Risks can include infringement on intellectual property, release of private information on individuals, libel, false advertising, and any other number of issues. This list is by no means exhaustive, but it should serve as a starting point when considering the legal issues that should be addressed in a social media policy.

For example, we are beginning to discuss with clients the concept of brand protection and protection against false and misleading statements. Many companies are unaware that a blog, Facebook message, or a tweet might contain statements that are potentially harmful to the company and could also infringe upon a trademark or a service mark. Keeping track of that type of information is key for today's executives.

Q: What discussions are lawyers and law firms having in regard to social media's impact on the legal profession?

A: This is probably one of the most commonly discussed issues in legal journals these days. For example, litigators are using social media to do research on opposing parties and claimants, particularly in employment and personal injury type cases. No longer do you need to pay the high-priced private investigator to film the plaintiff claiming a severe physical injury playing tennis. Now, you simply need to find him discussing his great tennis game on Facebook or in a tweet. Similarly, corporate lawyers are using social media as an extension of the Internet in conducting due diligence in business transactions.

There is also substantial discussion concerning safety and privacy concerns for attorneys' own personal information. Information about individuals can be found on firm or business Web pages, and now people can literally track individuals. Some may tweet what they are doing and others may even participate on Foursquare, which identifies physical location. It seems that many of the young professionals who grew up with this technology are less concerned about their personal privacy issues than are older individuals.

We also find ourselves addressing the "speed versus accuracy" problems with respect to social media. We all know how poorly most of us type an e-mail. We now are typing with our thumbs and often with little thought. This can be dangerous for lawyers. Clients have a desire for instantaneous information, and many expect their lawyers to be available on an almost 24/7 basis. In 1997 I was required by a client to purchase a home fax machine so that he could forward documents to me at whatever hour. Not surprisingly, it has been years since a client has even asked me for my home fax number. We have entered a new era. Helping our lawyers balance the requested speed with the required accuracy is an important challenge for the modern law firm that wants to avoid malpractice claims.

Finally, law firms have been concerned for years about offering advice on the Internet. For example, many firms have been slow to adopt blogs and even the posting of client alerts on topical issues. We need to balance the concern about whether an attorney-client relationship is being developed against the desire to market and put information in front of clients and potential clients as soon as possible. Social media makes it easy to have conversations with people who may not know the ground rules and might assume that a relationship may exist where it really does not.

Q: Can you give some examples of how social media might impact corporate governance?

A: Public companies have a particular issue with information finding its way into the market prematurely.

The Securities and Exchange Commission is looking into this issue and is creating rules to be sure that information is fairly available in the marketplace. Is a tweet on an account with 1,000 followers disclosure to the market? Probably not, but as the usage of social media becomes more prevalent, these methods of distributing information will become more commonplace. Recently, Google announced a change in senior management. Not only did they file the traditional form with the Securities and Exchange Commission, but within eight seconds of the filing, they also posted a tweet with the exact same information. Google probably knows something, and that is that many of the people following their stock are following on Twitter because it is a quicker method for finding out what is happening within the company.

While public companies may have the greatest challenge with respect to social media and the issues surrounding disclosure, all companies need to be developing rational policies with respect to social media and how it delivers information concerning the company into the marketplace.

Companies should adopt and distribute effective policies governing employees' usage of the company's computer system and employees' use of public forums to disseminate potentially confidential client and company information. Policies should advise employees that their use of a company system is subject to being monitored. This will help to reduce potential liability for employee privacy claims.

Also, companies should consider revising their electronic communication policies to be more specific. The policies should be broad enough to include all forms of electronic communication, including social media sites, instant messaging, Web postings, chat rooms, bulletin boards, and YouTube.com, for example, while balancing an employee's rights to use the sites. Implementing effective policies, along with consistent enforcement and application, will help protect employers.

A company might also consider revisions to their policies to cover smartphones and other personal uses of social media outside of work hours. Such revisions can be as simple as including a reference to "an employees' personal website or blog" in the Internet and Computer Use Policy and possibly in the Anti-Harassment Policy. Alternatively, companies may decide to supplement their current policies with a freestanding policy on employee use of social media.

The SEC hasn't been slow in coming to social media. They have a Twitter account with more than 160,000 followers. And they pay attention. In June 2011, they entered into a cease and desist order with two advertising executives who tried to raise $300 million to buy Pabst Brewing through Facebook and Twitter messages. Although they offered the would-be investors a bonus equal to beer of an equal value to their investment, the SEC still insisted on proper registration of offerings.

Q: What do you want to achieve with your social media programs and how do you view costs versus benefits of social media?

A: We want to use social media to increase contact with our clients. Business and marketing consultants are always telling you that the more "touches" that you have with a client or prospective client, the greater the likelihood of developing business. Social media outlets allow us to increase touches in both quantity and quality. This is particularly true for a firm like ours, which has multiple offices. All in all, our desire is to build relationships and partnerships with clients, not just to provide legal services. Many of our clients have been with us for decades and the goal is to develop more of those long-term relationships.

The costs of social media are probably more potential than actual. It's hard to quantify, for example, the real cost of an employee inadvertently distributing confidential information, or the amount of time and productivity lost with employees on social media sites. The benefits, on the other hand, are even less clear, particularly in the short run. The ability to put information into the hands of prospective clients, the ability to raise awareness of your business, as well as the ability to market and put the information into the correct hands are all potential benefits. With the help of companies like Social Strategy1, we are beginning to identify what benefits are available to our firm and to our clients, and more directly identify the costs.

I am very grateful to Ed for taking time to provide such comprehensive and thoughtful answers to my questions. It's evident that he recognizes the need for thought leadership initiatives for his firm and clients to keep pace with the changes being brought about by social media.

Our legal advisers, however, aren't the only professionals looking at the potential effects of social media beyond sales and marketing. The financial pros are paying attention, too.

Financial Reporting

Even if ours is not a public company, our own finance and accounting staffs, as well as outside audit firms, deal with many of the regulations brought about by Sarbanes-Oxley legislation. Each year, our independent auditors require us to provide them with as much information as possible on not only the prior year's operating results but also on developing trends of our business. Given the heightened regulatory and reporting requirements, it's not a huge reach to assume that as our businesses adopt online listening and monitoring applications, our collective financial and audit teams will want to be kept aware of trends and information that might have a material impact on our financial results. Examples of these trend-revealing questions might include:

- Are consumers acknowledging a shift to our competitors for reasons of price or other benefits?
- Are our competitors seeing meaningful declines in their business that might impact us? (Are new technologies, for example, causing a shift?)
- Is any portion of our company's online presence creating a meaningful financial impact (favorable or unfavorable)?

These are just a few areas about where auditors will want to be informed before issuing their final audit report. With the availability of online listening and monitoring tools and solutions, the auditor's ability to validate management's direction is greatly increased. At

Social Strategy1, we are already seeing indications that this is becoming a routine part of the financial audit process, and our team is actively engaged with companies and their auditors to fulfill this need with a minimum of time, effort, and additional costs.

While the potential impact of social media on reporting to our directors and shareholders is probably not the primary consideration when we think of our social media strategy, I would argue that companies should be proactive in communicating their social media presence to their boards and stockholders. Including the results of social media and reputation management initiatives will be helpful in satisfying these constituents and establishing that management is aware of how the business is trending.

Industry-Specific Regulatory Guidelines

Among the industries with specific regulatory issues regarding social media policy are legal services, healthcare, and financial services. For hospitals, the primary concern is ensuring compliance with the Health Insurance Portability and Accountability Act (HIPAA), which protects patients' privacy rights. HIPAA guidelines for social media outreach compliance are quite straightforward: don't identify patients by name or upload photos or video of them to social sites without a signed consent form.[41] For the pharmaceutical industry, regulated by the FDA, things are a bit more complicated. Two FDA regulations have special application to social media advertising. "Adverse event" reporting requirements state that when pharmaceutical or medical device companies encounter descriptions of side effects by users of their products, they must report the incident to the FDA.[42] "Fair balance" guidelines require pharmaceutical companies to describe adverse side effects in fair balance with the description of good, intended effects of a drug. (Thanks, FDA, we love those TV commercials.)

For financial services concerns the recent Dodd-Frank legislation combined with other established regulations, has created a more complex social media policy environment. The Financial Industry Regulatory Authority (FINRA) publishes guidelines for financial services firms relating to blogs and social networking websites.[43]

For the rest of us, FTC guidelines recommend that companies limit their legal liabilities by (1) requiring disclosure and truthfulness in social media outreach; (2) monitoring the conversation and correcting misstatements; and (3) creating social media policies and training programs.[44]

Record Retention Policies

For many industries, there are also specific regulatory requirements for archiving of social media records. FINRA, for example, has recently issued guidelines for brokers and dealers. I expect we'll see more regulation coming forth as corporate use of social media expands. Without more specific guidance, however, the salient point here is that even a tweet is considered to be a business communication. If you are charged in a criminal or civil case, all social media content is subject to subpoena.

For purposes of e-discovery or litigation cases, the Federal Rules of Evidence require a digital timestamp and signature to authenticate electronic files. You must be able to prove the exact content of your social media pages from any given date. Given the rapid change inherent in social media, many companies may need to update their record retention strategies to satisfy requirements for digital evidence in court. This may involve preserving social media pages in their native format with the ability to replay them as if they were live. Social media records are now business records, and we shouldn't underestimate the value of preserving them.

Employee Use Policies

A big concern of business leaders today involves the crafting of policies for the use of social media by their own employees. Companies are recognizing the complexities of social media and realizing that employee engagement can have both positive and negative consequences. As we suggested in Chapter 7, it's valuable to communicate your social media goals and activities throughout your organization to obtain as much buy-in from your personnel as possible. An important part of this process is establishing effective social media guidelines to encourage and facilitate the right kind of employee involvement while preventing employee activities that are harmful or counterproductive.

This is easier said than done. Every organization is different, and certain industries have their own regulations and restrictions to consider. Again, there's no "one size fits all" template that will do the job.

I personally believe that it's completely unrealistic to attempt to completely control employee activity on social media sites and platforms. Employees will be active online for business and personal reasons. That's a good thing. We don't want to miss the benefits that our own employees might offer us in advocating for our brands, safeguarding our reputations, identifying new prospects and customers, or recruiting top talent for your organization. On the other hand, we don't want employees wasting their days chatting online with friends, shopping for shoes, or watching cute kitten videos. Social media has undoubtedly become a new workplace distraction. So was the telephone, once upon a time. Yet most employers long ago found a happy medium between a highly restrictive (Absolutely no personal phone calls at work!) policy and one where anything goes. We had to find that happy medium again when the Internet wired our workplaces. I have to believe we can do it again with Facebook.

I don't mean to minimize the complexities of social networking or the very real financial and legal risks for some businesses. The issues raised by Ed Brown in our preceding Q&A session should be reviewed for inclusion in setting your company's policies. I do believe, however, that with good policy messaging, and perhaps a little training, most companies can find a middle ground between policies that protect your company and those that allow your employees and partners to be enthusiastic advocates and ambassadors.

Here then, in very broad strokes, are the ideas that I believe can be successfully communicated to the employees of any organization of any size.

Keep Personal Access to a Minimum

The concept that work is work and play is play probably needs to be reiterated in regard to social media usage. Particularly so for those companies which have an active and dynamic social media strategy and some employees who engage in it as part of their job descriptions. Most companies should limit access to postings on behalf of the company (e.g., the company Facebook page or Twitter account) to approved employees anyway.

Your company may already have a written communications policy. Remind your employees that it covers social media, too, and then trust them to know the difference between use and abuse. Even tweeting about "what a great place this is to work" is inappropriate if you should be doing something else.

Distinguish Between Personal and Business Use

Activities like blogging, tweeting, or participating in discussion forums for work should be distinct from personal engagement. If the engagement is work-related, then employees should recognize the importance of directing their online activities to the benefit of the company and its customers. Employees should never attribute their personal engagement to professional representation or imply the authority to speak on behalf of the company with screen names, trademarks, or logos.

While all that may sound clear-cut enough, this is actually the tough one. The boundary between our personal lives and our professional lives is another one of those lines that social media is blurring. It can be quite disturbing for personnel to discover that in talking about their workplace, on their own time, and among their own friends, they are still representing the company.

The unfortunate truth is that many of the notorious public relations disasters that have caused brand damage (and employee termination or resignation) were not the result of deliberate maliciousness, but of tired or disgruntled individuals venting after a hard day's work. There was the Massachusetts teacher who called her community parents "snobby and arrogant." There was the Chrysler associate who complained about traffic in Detroit and dropped the f-bomb. There have been many other cases like these that can enliven training discussions and provide powerful examples of how fluid the concept of privacy is becoming.

Your training session should remind your employees that social media networking sites can change their privacy settings without notice. It might also remind them that your own monitoring and listening endeavors can pick up on their comments, too.

Protect Confidential Information and Trade Secrets

Policy should clearly prohibit employees from disclosing confidential proprietary information and trade secrets. This includes pricing, the names of, and information about customers, partners, suppliers, affiliates, or partnerships. Employee handbooks and confidentiality agreements likely cover these sensitive areas already, but the reach of social networking sites makes us all much more vulnerable.

Represent the Company Honestly

Encourage employees to be clear about their identities and their roles. They should disclose their affiliation with the company in any discussion of company products or services. While there's a difference of opinion on this, I would discourage the use of dual or bifurcated identities for home and work use. The Whole Foods incident described in Chapter 4 is just one example of how using this deception to "help" a company actually harmed it more.

Observe the Company's Established Code of Conduct and Good Business Practices

The social media spaces can be very casual environments and there's definitely a less buttoned-down style to communications. But that difference in style is not a difference in values. Our business leaders, our corporate cultures, and our corporate codes of conduct and other published documents already communicate our values. If we provide the leadership and guidance, most employees can willingly accept the basic conduct policies that apply to everyone.

Personally, I have a lot of faith in my own employees and trust them not to post anything off-color, disrespectful, or abusive—anything they wouldn't say to their mothers or the boss. I certainly don't want to squelch their ability to engage in social media conversations. On this point, I wholeheartedly agree with Scott Monty, head of social media at Ford Motor Company. When asked how companies can keep their employees from doing stupid things online, Monty had this to say:

> The same way it can keep employees from doing stupid things on email and the phone. Give them guidelines and resources. Have an online communications policy that follows standard communications policies and trust them to do the right thing.[45]

Conclusion

Social media won't be limited to just the sales and marketing teams. Already it's influencing how we manage our financial reporting, regulatory compliance, corporate governance, and human resources activities, and we can expect that it will increasingly alter day-to-day operations across the entire organization. Fortunately, the new listening and monitoring technologies can help us not only to deal with these changes, but also to have better insights ourselves into the directions our businesses are trending.

There are definitely legal risks to engaging in social media. New laws are evolving rapidly, and there's still a lot of gray area surrounding many issues. But business has always entailed risks. Sufficient knowledge and good practices can more than offset those risks, allowing honest and ethical businesses all the opportunities that social media affords.

Finally, when it comes to setting policy, I believe that our first acknowledgement has to be that our employees have free will and minds of their own. If we create policies that are impossibly restrictive, or try to be the Facebook police, we'll quash the enthusiasm and support of our best advocates. I'm convinced that if policy, messaging, and training are handled well, our employees will benefit from a much better understanding of how to manage their own personal social media activity and, in turn, help us to avoid future issues for the company. That's a win/win all the way around.

Chapter 11. The Future for Social Media

As I write this chapter at 33,000 feet, on my way home from a conference where social media and commerce were the big areas of conversation, I am full of ideas on what the future has in store. Predictions are very tricky and so often wrong, and yet as businesspeople, we have to think ahead and make real financial bets. If we don't, our companies stagnate and we give up the benefits of growth and profits to those who do take calculated risks and make the right calls.

As an entrepreneur, this is most likely part of my DNA, so I'm accustomed to guessing what's over the next hill and trying to figure out what to do if I guess right. That can be difficult with social media. A little like trying, in 1880, to prognosticate about the long-term effects of the Industrial Revolution. Or guessing, in 1980, about how the Internet might change our lives. The social media revolution has occurred so rapidly, and has already made such enormous changes in the way we communicate, collaborate, and network, that it's really impossible to predict into a very distant future.

Some trends, however, have already been set in motion. Some near-term evolutions are revealing themselves that I think will almost immediately impact the future of our businesses as well as our private lives. With that said, here I go with ideas and predictions that I believe will soon be important to your future and the future of your business.

1. The evolution of smartphones and tablet devices will greatly expand social media usage and applications.

I can almost hear the groaning over this obvious prediction, but a book on social media would not be complete without a discussion of the impact that will evolve from this trend. As a matter of fact, I'm not sure that most people actually realize how far-reaching and pervasive the shift to smart devices really is.

The mobile market is teaching us that we have become genuinely Web-dependent and don't function very well without connectivity. On a recent trip to London, my son discovered that it was difficult to access Wi-Fi and that his mobile phone was mostly useless in the city's underground Tube system. He returned to learn that the city of London had just announced plans to have widespread Wi-Fi throughout the subway system by 2012. Many other European, Canadian, and US cities have already launched municipal Wi-Fi and many more have plans on the drawing board. Urban areas already offer enough service from cafés, shops, and hotels to make dead zones, like London's Tube system, the exception rather than the rule, and the era of ubiquitous Wi-Fi, at least in cities, is not very far off.

The availability of Wi-Fi on mobile phones is driving the use of Wi-Fi networks across the country, and many of us already take for granted that wireless technology is an essential part of our daily work flow. Those travelers among you who can remember standing in line to grab an airport payphone to check messages before a flight can appreciate what this means. And how many of us today would even consider checking into a hotel that didn't offer wireless access?

With more than 80% of the American population now owning a mobile phone—and many people now owning two or more mobile devices—the explosion of text messaging, social shopping, and mobile commerce in general is well underway. The acceleration of the development of mobile payment methods and mobile apps is almost difficult to comprehend.

Since its launch in 2010, Apple's iPad has sold more than 20 million units and even with supply chain problems, Apple insiders forecast shipments of just under 40 million units for 2011. With other tablet devices hitting the market, too, you get the picture. Here are a few more eye-opening stats:

- Global mobile data traffic grew 2.6-fold in 2010, nearly tripling for the third year in a row.
- Last year's mobile data traffic was three times the size of the entire global Internet in 2000.
- Average smartphone usage doubled in 2010.
- Smartphones represent only 13 percent of the total global handsets in use today, but they represent more than 78% of total global handset traffic.
- In 2010 three million tablet devices were connected to the mobile network, and each tablet generated 5 times more traffic than the average smartphone.
- There are 48 million people in the world who have mobile phones, even though they don't have electricity at home. The mobile network has extended beyond the boundaries of the power grid.

The potential in mobile advertising for large

businesses is obvious, but it may be that among the biggest beneficiaries of this trend will be small businesses and also the urban public. One of the benefits of mobile use and geolocation advertising is that it has the potential for regenerating interests in local neighborhoods. I predict that the location-based services of the immediate future will become more narrowly focused, as people begin to use these services for specific and personal value in the neighborhoods where they live and work.

Social media will grow with mobile use and vice versa. We all need to align our businesses to this trend.

2. Social Media will alter, not replace traditional media.

For some time now, a number of social media prognosticators have been predicting that social media will eventually replace traditional media, or reduce it to near irrelevance. It's true that overall media spend is shifting from traditional media (print, radio, TV, etc.) to social media. This shift will continue for the near term as more and more companies test the waters of social media marketing. I don't think, however, that this current dynamic is permanent, or that it predicts a quick demise for traditional media. I expect that we'll quickly find a point of equilibrium and harmony will reign between old and new media.

My reason for saying this is not hard to understand. As companies see how prospects and customers respond to blogs, Facebook pages, online listening and monitoring, and all the other applications we've discussed, it seems logical that they will incorporate the information and data they obtain into traditional advertising programs. Wouldn't you spend more on TV, print, or radio if you knew that the message you were projecting was already being well received by your online followers?

The truth is that, with the exception of newspapers, traditional media is still quite healthy and it's already begun to make major adaptations to the new listening and reading habits of online users. Radio, whose demise was predicted with the invention of television, and again when cable TV came along, has seen its weekly online radio audience double every five years since 2001. Online radio now reaches an estimated 57 million people age twelve and older per week.[46] Portable listening devices like the iPad and Zune are doing their part to ensure that radio transitions into the digital age, and I'm confident that radio will continue to be a media survivor.

In television, too, we're seeing a merger in consumption. Last year's Super Bowl, the most viewed

TV show in history, was also the subject of a Twitter-breaking record. I don't think it's coincidence that the top social media shows, like *American Idol* and *Dancing with the Stars*, also top the Nielsen's list for most viewers.

After some slump years, when their viewers were glued more solidly to their PCs than they were to their TV sets, television networks are starting to capitalize on social media platforms to lure some of those viewers back. This spring CBS launched "Tweetweek," an eight-night week during which viewers could log into their Twitter account to watch some of their favorite actors, musicians, and sports analysts tweet live during the broadcast of their respective programs. Throughout the shows, fans were given firsthand commentary and the opportunity to submit questions. I don't know yet how the experiment went for CBS. But I think it's a great example of the creative thinking that will not only save television, but also generate new marketing opportunities for sponsors by allowing viewer comment and participation. Not only will this approach have a positive impact on viewer ratings, but it will allow sponsors to have access to data that can be analyzed and evaluated using the metrics tools we discussed in the previous chapter.

There's also exciting talk out there about "second

screen" technologies, built initially on iPads and extended to the plethora of devices we'll see over the next few years. Nobody has a crystal ball, but some things seem self-evident. We're definitely going to consume more TV in the palms of our hands. We'll see a lot more cross-messaging between social media and television, and ad dollars will flow both ways.

The situation for print media, for magazines and newspapers, is a bit darker, but I think there's hope there, too. As newspapers, radio, and TV develop their own multimedia strategies, they'll create new experiences for online and offline consumers alike. And as businesses get better at integrating social media and traditional marketing efforts, I'm optimistic that we'll create collaborations that will keep everyone in business.

3. Social networks will become portable.

A frequently heard complaint about social media platforms is that they tend to be "walled gardens," shut off from the rest of the Web. Users of these sites are obliged to maintain separate accounts on the variety of social networks they use. Every blog, photo and video sharing site, bookmarking, shopping, or gaming app requires a new login, password, and profile creation and the necessity for "re-friending" social connections. This is a real pain for active Internet users, and a pain for developers, too. The unique application user interfaces (APIs) that each of these sites is built on necessarily forces developers to write separate applications for each of these walled gardens.

For some time now I've sensed considerable pressure on social networks to tear down those walls, or at least to make networking more open and portable, and there's a lot of movement in that direction. Google has pioneered Open Social, a set of common APIs for building social applications across the Web. According to Google's Press Center, the sites that have already committed to supporting Open Social (including Engage.com, LinkedIn, MySpace, Ning, Oracle, Salesforce.com and XING, to name a few) already represent an audience of about 200 million users globally.[47]

Others are also working on open social networking standards and even Mark Zuckerberg, the ultimate walled gardener, has opened up a bit. Facebook Connect, launched in December 2008, is a network of more than ten thousand independent sites that allows Facebook users to use their friend's details. In April 2009 Facebook launched Open Stream API, which allows you to see friends' newsfeeds from any site. More recently, Facebook has offered other online entities the chance to outsource the handling of their comments, too.

When users want to comment, they log in to Facebook, which hosts the posts.

While any of these moves might be perceived as further reflections of Facebook's goal of web dominance, I see them as strong evidence of this growing pressure to open those garden gates. And I'm not the only one with this perspective.

Making his own predictions on the future of social networking at the end of 2010, Mark Suster had this to say:

> Right now our social graph (whom we are connected to and their key information like email addresses) is mostly held captive by Facebook. There is growing pressure on Facebook to make this portable and they have made some progress on this front. Ultimately, I don't believe users or society as a whole will accept a single company "locking in" our vital information.
>
> Facebook will succumb to pressure and over time make this available to us to allow us more choice in being part of several social networks without having to spam all of our friends again. I know in 2010 this doesn't seem obvious to everybody, but it's my judgment. Either they make our social graph portable or we'll find other networks to join. I predict this

will come before the end of 2012.[48]

I'm not sure that I'm willing to go out on a limb quite that time-specific, but I do agree with Suster that the portable social graph is inevitable. Many streams are converging to bring us a less centralized, more open style of social networking in the very near future.

The implications of this movement for businesses are enormous. Users will be able to move between networks more quickly, without checking in, and they'll take their profile, their friends, and their portable shopping carts with them. It will be much easier to gain access to the vast social media ecosystem even from our own company websites. Development speed will escalate, getting useful and innovative features to users much faster and opening a floodgate of social features and new marketing opportunities in contexts we haven't even thought of.

4. Ratings, rankings, and reviews will rule.

I've already devoted considerable attention in these pages to the importance of user-generated ratings, rankings, and reviews, but this phenomena, like the mobile explosion, is still underestimated by far too many. This big trend will only get bigger. Third-party review sites will continue to proliferate, user reviews will grow in importance to search engine algorithms, and consumers will continue to seek out trusted recommendations before buying.

Those companies that derive real competitive advantage from these dynamics will need to be laser-focused on new ways to facilitate and to use more user-generated conversation. They'll increase their use of listening and monitoring tools to identify more customer chatter surrounding ratings, rankings, and reviews, and they'll use that information to produce quality sales leads and consequently, positive ROI.

In our own work with clients, we are on a rapid learning curve to use search applications as a way to identify and interact with prospects who are making their needs and wants known online. The recent acquisition of the social media monitoring platform Radian6 by Salesforce.com is solid proof that online monitoring will be combined with the process of identifying and selling to prospects.

There is little question that companies will have to become aggressive and innovative in finding ways to conduct ratings and rankings discussions on their own sites as well as other social sites like Facebook. Twitter already represents a great application for following conversations that provide ratings and reviews, but it will also be a great channel through which to stimulate these same conversations and even route the conversation to your site. In addition, the geolocal platforms, like Foursquare, are great sources for encouraging these conversations. Smartphones, tablets, and the like will increase the volume, but we'll have to be aggressive in identifying new sources of this information and in developing ways to follow and engage with consumers as they appear in new places.

5. Social media will become mainstreamed throughout the organization.

Research currently shows that Human Resources, Finance, Production, R&D, many areas of management, and other departments are usually left out of social media initiatives, particularly when organizations take a trial balloon or campaign-by-campaign approach. I expect that this will change rapidly over the next few years as companies begin to realize, from their own experience and that of others, that they can't harness the power of social media unless there is full organizational engagement.

For some companies, this may mean significant cultural change and a serious assessment of how the organization will move into the social, collaborative Web. Corporate silos and one-way, top-down communication models strangle the potential that resides in social media. Mainstreaming, or institutionalizing, social media across the organization is the only possible way to have rapid-response strategies for evolving, real-time conversations.

I'm very optimistic that business leaders are starting to grasp, much faster, the fact that social media affects not just the marketing and PR departments, but recruiting, customer service, sales, community relations, and more. As we saw in Chapter 10, the finance and legal staffs of many firms are already deeply involved in its legal and financial implications. In most organizations, every function and department will have some involvement or relationship with social media.

As more companies begin to see that social media is central to the entire business strategy, they'll elevate or bring on C-suite executives for social media management. In larger companies, you are going to see more designations like Chief Listening Officer and probably responsibilities delegated on a brand-by-brand basis, too.

While doing social media well does require a sound knowledge of traditional marketing, managing social media calls for a set of very different marketing techniques. This is forcing organizations to hire social media specialists, and we're already starting to see new and interesting designations being coined, like Social Media Strategist, Social Media Campaign Manager,

Social Media Analyst, Online Community Manager, and Content Development Manager. A parallel development is the increasing demand for specialized training and education in social media. Some pioneering business schools, like Wharton, are already offering courses in social media marketing as a part of the MBA curriculum. As more companies mainstream social media, recognizing its relevance to many organizational areas, I think we'll see this trend take on much more momentum and importance.

6. Facebook will get more competition.

You'll notice that I've phrased this one cautiously. I'm not about to predict the demise of Zuckerberg's brainchild. I don't expect a lemming-like abandonment of Facebook. I do see, now that so many of us have been initiated to social networking, and as the technologies for creating new social applications become more accessible, that more users will gravitate to smaller, specialized social networks where the sharing centers narrowly on professional or personal interests.

The growth in niche networks had been underway for a while now, but the new burst is coming from the horde of companies who are providing custom social networks, hosted do-it-yourself solutions, or downloadable software for building your own social network. It just follows that, as it becomes easier and more economical to build your own network, niche networks will continue to proliferate. (Ning alone now has 90,000 paid subscribers.)

While many of these new networks won't make it, a lot of them will, as users seek a more specialized social experience. These subsets of Facebook, while smaller, have tremendous potential for marketers because they can generate intense consumer engagement, acting as lead-qualified vertical markets for some products and services. They'll also put more demand on our monitoring tools for scouring the entirety of the Web to stay on top of these newly developing sites.

7. Watch for the rise of social search.

I had originally planned to mention social search as an extension of the discussion on user-generated ratings, rankings, and reviews, but since I began drafting this chapter, two announcements have appeared that convinced me that the ascendance of social search should be its own prediction. Last week Bing announced that it will be integrating Facebook data into its searches in a significant way. For users logged in to Facebook, Bing will pull in your friends' Likes, actually reordering the search results so that your friend's recommendations will influence the Ten Blue Links. Following hard on that bit of news, Google's Search Blog officially announced the global rollout of its Social Search engine in nineteen new languages. Social search is arriving even faster than I anticipated.

It's going to be a mixed bag for social search for a while. Initial results are mixed, and most of us will see more content from strangers than from real friends. But social search has the potential to really shake up SEO practices, making traditional keywords much less important than recommendations from those we know. The search experience will more closely parallel the way we seek information in real life, by first questioning our family members, peers, and other social connections.

As the tools get better, and as more social signals like tweets and mobile app check-ins become assimilated into them, we'll see social search grow in importance. This trend definitely means that brands will have to become more social.

8. Privacy and identity issues will dominate the decade.

In July of 1993, a cartoon drawn by Peter Steiner and published by *The New Yorker* depicted two dogs sitting in front of a computer. The cartoon's caption read, "On the Internet no one knows you're a dog." The now-famous cartoon became a symbol for the freedom that the Internet gave users for sending messages anonymously or for creating alter identities that were significantly different from their true ones.

Almost two decades later, accustomed as we are to hearing about cases of cyberstalking, Internet bullying, and identity theft, Steiner's cartoon seems a little less funny. It's certainly a lot less true. In fact, an Internet social search company in China now uses the phrase, "On the Internet, *everybody* knows you're a dog," emphasizing the human effort-collaborated exposure and mass distribution of personal information. And by now we've all read enough, or seen enough TV episodes, to know that "they" really can rout you out if you're up to no good.

The idea of being unable to hide our "dogginess," however, is troubling for many people. Anonymous or false identities don't necessarily conceal criminal or unethical intent. They often provide polite cover for commentary on sexual orientation, for political leanings, or religious differences that would make the user unpopular at home or at work. The loss of anonymity online could also be a serious setback for marginalized populations or activists in autocratic governments.

But the arc of the online universe is bending toward authenticity and I believe that using our true identities online will become the norm. An interesting appraisal and perhaps a good indicator of this trend comes from Facebook. The following excerpt from *The Economist* is telling:

> At last an effective troll-busting weapon is at hand: Facebook. The world's biggest social network, which now boasts more than 500m members, insists that people use their real names. Having more than one identity, argues Mark Zuckerberg, the firm's founder, "is an example of a lack of integrity." Most Facebook members comply voluntarily because they want to deal with real friends, not fake ones.[49]

Whether or not they buy Zuckerberg's reasoning, there are lots of others who'd like to be sure that you're not only human, but the human you say you are. Given the trillions of dollars already moving annually through e-commerce transactions, businesses have an enormous stake in identity authentication. For government, identity and security issues are central to its ability to fight cybercrime, foster economic growth, and promote representative democracy. Personally, I look forward to the day that we can vote from our computers. It won't happen, though, as long as my dog can cast the same ballot.

For these (and more serious) reasons, the federal government has just issued a framework strategy document entitled *The National Strategy for Trusted Identities in Cyberspace*. The aspirations of the NSTIC are so important that technology writer Alex Howard has called it the "Manhattan Project for online identity."[50] The NSTIC doesn't advocate for any specific solutions or call for citizen identities or a national ID card (although information cards may well be one of the trusted sources for online identity in the future, along with smartphones and other physical tokens). Rather it calls on the nation's innovators to get busy, creating better methods for trusted identity and authentication.

The issues of privacy and security are complex and intermingled. There's no easy solution here, but it behooves businesses to keep a watchful eye. I expect to see new laws coming down the pike that will hold companies more accountable for online security breaches either through comprehensive cyber security legislation, or through HR 2221, the Data Accountability and Trust Act (DATA) that passed the US House of Representatives this year. And businesses themselves need updated laws and good information to avoid lawsuits, government intervention, and loss of customers. The status quo won't last. Expect the debates to heat up.

9. More, more, more.

There is an entire cluster of "safe" bets on the

future of social media that will bring us full circle to our "Chatter That Matters" discussion from Chapter 2. The chatter is going to matter even more. As we see more broadband and Wi-Fi, more online time spent by users, more globalization of social media, more user communities and networks, and much more mobile use, it will quickly become almost impossible to remember "the way we were." I especially expect to see a rise in social activism and an even greater influence of social media on politics. Social media has the potential for becoming the ultimate grassroots, the biggest town hall on the planet. Watch for the big battles in next year's presidential election to be waged in social networks. Generally, I feel very comfortable in predicting that social media will play a greater part in the day-to-day life of every one of us.

Conclusion

Prognosticating is always fun, even though it can be a little humiliating when we review it with 20/20 hindsight. I hope that in a few years most of my predictions will have proven accurate, but I know that technology, and human behavior, can always surprise us.

The main goal of this book was to share our own experiences and some best practices in social media in the hope that these might serve as both resource and inspiration for those of you who are seriously contemplating social media strategies.

In ILD's first fifteen years, we've been successful because we have always attempted to evolve and grow to keep up with changes in markets and technology. Our emphasis on social media is constantly growing, and if properly managed, we hope it will add another fifteen years of success for us. Regardless of how we fare, the game has changed in ways none of us can ignore.

The future success of social media enterprises will not be determined as much by their ability to create new technologies, but from understanding the way we as groups and individuals seek information, collaborate, and transact for goods and services on a local, national, and global basis. As the Web grows more and more social in nature, all of us must get a better handle on just how fundamentally relationships between customers and businesses have changed. For businesses that embrace this change, and work to discover ways to benefit from it, the future holds promise. For those who continue to wait and watch, the future may be a little less rewarding.

My guess is that you read this book because you had an interest in getting into the game or enhancing your existing game. With the potential of 3 billion people online this year, it's a great game to join! Don't be intimidated by the technology, terminology, or new metrics. These can all be mastered. Focus on what you want to accomplish and look for the right places to join the conversation and the right ways to find and engage with customers and prospects.

My uncle Charlie always told me that there are two kinds of people in the world: wishers and doers. We are all at the point of deciding which one of these we will become as the world around us changes faster than ever. It may be time to move from the wishing phase and get on with the doing part. At some point, it's time to stop the evaluation process and get off the bench and into the game. I hope you decide that time is now. You can't win if you don't play!

Notes

Chapter 2

[1]Seshadri Tirunillai and Gerard J. Tellis, "Does Chatter Really Matter? User Generated Content and Stock Performance," May 31, 2011, available at Social Science Research Network, http://ssrn.com/abstract=1856482.

[2]"The Internet and Campaign 2010." Pew Internet and American Life Project. March 17, 2011, http://www.pewinternet.org/~/media//Files/Repor ts/2011/Internet%20and%20Campaign%202010. pdf.

[3]"Global Publics Embrace Social Networking," Pew Global Attitudes Project. December 15, 2010, http://pewresearch.org/pubs/1830/social-networking-computer-cell-phone-usage-around-the-world.

[4]Katharine Viner, "Internet Has Changed Foreign Policy Forever, Says Gordon Brown," *Guardian*, June 19, 2009, http://www.guardian.co.uk/politics/2009/jun/19/g ordon-brown-internet-foreign-policy.

[5]Jennifer Van Grove, "Red Cross Raises $5,000,000+ for
     Haiti Through Text Message Campaign,"
     Mashable, January 13, 2010,
     http://mashable.com/2010/01/13/haiti-red-cross-
     donations/.

[6]http://www.charitywater.org/.

Chapter 3

[7]Brett Borders, "A Brief History of Social Media," June
     2, 2009, http://socialmediarockstar.com/history-
     of-social-media.

[8]Dave Harkins, "Why We Need Social Media," July 8,
     2009, http://www.davidharkins.com/social-
     media/.

[9]Tom Hayes, *Jump Point: How Network Culture is
     Revolutionizing Business* (New York: McGraw-
     Hill Companies, 2008), xi.

[10]Peter Corbett. "Facebook Demographics and Statistics
     Report 2010: 145% Growth in 1 Year,"
     iStrategyLabs, January 4, 2010,
     http://www.istrategylabs.com/2010/01/facebook-
     demographics-and-statistics-report-2010-145-
     growth-in-1-year/.

[11]"Global Publics Embrace Social Networking," Pew
     Global Attitudes Project. December 15, 2010,
     http://pewresearch.org/pubs/1830/social-
     networking-computer-cell-phone-usage-around-

the-world.

[12]Nora Ganim Barnes, Ph.D. "The 2010 Inc. 500 Update: Most Blog, Friend and Tweet but Some Industries Still Shun Social Media," The University of Massachusetts Dartmouth Center for Marketing Research, 2010. Full text available at http://www.umassd.edu/media/umassdartmouth/c mr/studiesandresearch/2010inc500.pdf.

[13]Digital Media Strategies, *Online Advertising: Global Market Forecast*, November 30, 2010.

[14]Jon Sobel, "State of the Blogosphere 2010," *Technorati*, November 3, 2010, http://technorati.com/blogging/article/state-of-the-blogosphere-2010-introduction/.

[15]T. M. Capital Corp., "Digital Media: Monetizing Social and Mobile Media Industry Spotlight," 2011, p. 8. Full text available at http://www.ibicorporatefinance.ie/files/2011/201 10331.pdf.

[16]Qtd. by Lori Taylor, "Why Social Media Gaming is Big Business for Your Business," *Social Media Examiner*, August 12, 2010, http://www.socialmediaexaminer.com/why-social-media-gaming-is-big-business-for-your-business/.

[17]T. M. Capital Corp., "Digital Media," p. 15.

Chapter 4

[18]"The Importance of Social Media in Making Business Decisions," *WebPort Global*, November 22, 2010, http://webportglobal.com/Blog-Community/Small-Army-Blog/November-2010/The-Importance-of-Social-Media-in-Making-Business-.aspx.

[19]Erik Qualman, *Socialnomics: How Social Media Transforms the Way We Live and Do Business.* (Hoboken, N.J.: John Wiley & Sons, Inc., 2009), viii.

[20]"Social Media Bites Whole Foods CEO," *Enterprise Web 2.0*, http://www.enterpriseweb2.com/?p=250.

[21]Palavi Gogoi, "Wal-mart's Jim and Laura: The Real Story," *Business Week*, October 9, 2006, http://www.businessweek.com/bwdaily/dnflash/content/oct2006/db20061009_579137.htm.

[22]Brian Morrisey, "Q&A: Zappos CEO Tony Hsieh," *Adweek*, December 22, 2008,http://www.adweek.com/news/advertising-branding/qa-zappos-ceo-tony-hsieh-97859?pn=2.

[23]Erica Swallow, "Best Social Media Customer Service Finalists Discuss Their Success," Mashable, December 9, 2010, http://mashable.com/2010/12/09/social-media-customer-service-finalists/.

[24]Casey Hibbard, "How Microsoft Xbox Uses Twitter to Reduce Support Costs," *Social Media Examiner*, July 27, 2010, http://www.socialmediaexaminer.com/how-microsoft-xbox-uses-twitter-to-reduce-support-costs/.

[25]Mack Collier, "5 Ways Companies are Using Social Media to Lower Costs,"mackcollier.com, http://mackcollier.com/5-ways-companies-are-using-social-media-to-lower-costs/.

[26]Jive Software Press Release, "Jive Survey Reveals Key Business Benefits from Social Business Adoption," January 31, 2011.Full text available at http://www.jivesoftware.com/news/releases/2011/1/jive-survey-reveals-key-business-benefits-from-social-business-adoption.

[27]Natalie L. Petouhoff, Ph.D., Connie Moore, Andrew Magarie, "Adding Social Media to Customer Service Initiatives Can Break Down Barriers to Change," Executive Summary, Forrester Research, February 11, 2010.

[28]Paul Gillin, *The New Influencers* (Fresno, Calif: Quill Driver Books, 2009), 4.

Chapter 5

[29]Mark Penn, "New Info Shoppers," *Wall Street Journal*, January 8, 2009, http://online.wsj.com/article/SB12314448300536

5353.html?mod=rss_media_and_marketing.

[30]Evelyn M. Rusli, "Gilt Groupe Chief Considering IPO in 2012," *New York Times*, February 18, 2011, http://dealbook.nytimes.com/2011/02/18/gilt-groupe-chief-considering-i-p-o-in-2012/?src=dlbksb.

[31]Max Chafkin. "You've Been Yelped," *Inc.*, February 2010. http://www.inc.com/magazine/20100201/youve-been-yelped.html.

[32]Robert Ball, "Groupon Gap Deal: What was the True Cost?" *Huffington Post*, January 12, 2011, http://www.huffingtonpost.com/robert-ball/group-buying-whats-the-tr_b_808121.html.

[33]Utpal M. Dholakia, "How Effective Are Groupon Promotions for Business?" September 28, 2010. Full text available at http://www.ruf.rice.edu/~dholakia/Groupon%20Effectiveness%20Study,%20Sep%2028%202010.pdf.

[34]Robert Ball, "Group Buying Versus Traditional Lead Generation," *Huffington Post*, January 25, 2011, http://www.huffingtonpost.com/robert-ball/group-buying-versus-tradi_b_813552.html.

Chapter 6

[35]Emily Steele. "Nestle Takes a Beating on Social-Media

Sites,"*Wall Street Journal*, March 29, 2010, http://online.wsj.com/article/SB10001424052702 30443440457514988385050815.html.

[36]Erica Swallow, "How to Use Social Media for Lead Generation," Mashable, June 24, 2010, http://mashable.com/2010/06/24/social-media-lead-generation/.

[37]Vanina Delobelle, Ph.D, "Social Media Strategy," May 2008, slide presentation athttp://www.slideshare.net/vaninadelobelle/social-media-strategy-392440.

[38]"The New Conversation: Taking Social Media from Talk to Action."A Harvard Business Review Analytic Services Report. Cambridge, Mass.: Harvard Business School, 2010.

Chapter 8

[39]"Users' Group," Wikipedia, http://en.wikipedia.org/wiki/Users_group.

[40]Richard Millington, "The Amateur Approach to Building Online Communities," *The Online Community Guide*, http://www.feverbee.com/2011/04/branded.html.

Chapter 10

[41]*Health Insurance Portability and Accountability Act of 1996*. Full text available at

http://www.gpo.gov/fdsys/pkg/CRPT-
104hrpt736/pdf/CRPT-104hrpt736.pdf.

[42]*Adverse Event Reporting System (AERS)*. Full text
available at
http://www.fda.gov/Drugs/GuidanceCompliance
RegulatoryInformation/Surveillance/AdverseDru
gEffects/default.htm.

[43]Financial Industry Regulatory Authority, Inc. "Social
Media Web Sites: Guidance on Blogs and Social
Networking Web Sites," 2010. Full text available
at
http://www.finra.org/web/groups/industry/@ip/@
reg/@notice/documents/notices/p120779.pdf

[44]Federal Trade Commission, 16 CFR Part 255, *Guide
Concerning the Use of Endorsements and
Testimonials in Advertising*, 2009. Full text
available at
http://www.ftc.gov/os/2009/10/091005endorseme
ntguidesfnnotice.pdf.

[45]"Lawsuits and PR Nightmares: Why Employees Need
Social Media Guidelines," *Search Engine
Journal*, August 19, 2009,
http://www.searchenginejournal.com/why-
employees-need-social-media-guidelines/12588/.

Chapter 11

[46]Arbitron study, "The Infinite Dial 2011: Navigating
Digital Platforms," available at

http://www.arbitron.com/study/digital_radio_stud y.asp.

[47]"Google Launches OpenSocial to Spread Social Applications Across the Web," November 1, 2007, http://www.google.com/intl/en/press/pressrel/ope nsocial.html.

[48]Mark Suster, "Social Networking: the Future," *Techcrunch,* December 5, 2010, http://techcrunch.com/2010/12/05/social-networking-future/.

[49]*The Economist,* "Trolling for your Soul: The Price of Civil Online Comments May Be More Power for Facebook," *The Economist,* March 31, 2011, http://www.economist.com/node/18483765?story _id=18483765.

[50]Alex Howard, "A Manhattan Project for Online Identity," *O'Reilly Radar*, May 4, 2011, http://radar.oreilly.com/2011/05/nstic-analysis-identity-privacy.html.

Index

"Many tools are emerging to help manage your reputation, but effective strategy should precede any technology." - Gartner

You need strategy, analysis, and you need experts...

You need Social Strategy1.

Socialstrategy1.com/socialmedialeadership

Products for large and small business

Join the growing client list discovering the value of real-time analysis across digital information networks and online conversations.

Gain exposure to the wider digital world, analyze the conversations, and sell and upsell to your prospects and those of your competitors.

Social media can help you make money.